APPRECIATING
OYSTERS

APPRECIATING OYSTERS

AN EATER'S GUIDE TO CRAFT OYSTERS
FROM TIDE TO TABLE

DANA DESKIEWICZ

THE COUNTRYMAN PRESS
A DIVISION OF W. W. NORTON & COMPANY
INDEPENDENT PUBLISHERS SINCE 1923

For information about permission to
reproduce selections from this book, write
to Permissions, The Countryman Press,
500 Fifth Avenue, New York, NY 10110

For information about special discounts
or bulk purchases, please contact:
W. W. Norton Special Sales at
specialsales@wwnorton.com
or 800-233-4830

Book design by Faceout Studio
Manufacturing through Asia Pacific Offset
Production manager: Devon Zahn

The Countryman Press
www.countrymanpress.com

A division of W. W. Norton & Company, Inc.
500 Fifth Avenue, New York, NY 10110
www.wwnorton.com

978-1-68268-094-0

0 9 8 7 6 5 4 3 2 1

FOR MAŁA AND DEEJ

CONTENTS

INTRODUCTION

HOW I LEARNED TO START GIVING A SHUCK AND LOVE THE OYSTER

"He was a bold man that first ate an oyster."

—*Jonathan Swift*

Close your eyes. Go ahead. It's OK. Now imagine you're sitting oceanside, a cool summer breeze drifting in off the waves. Subtle notes of salt and sweet seaweed waft into your nose. Goosebumps roll over your skin as you feel the sun hide behind a band of cumulus clouds.

This is how it feels to eat an oyster. In the culinary world, it's hard to match such a pure, simple experience as looking at an oyster, holding it, and putting it in your mouth. These intriguing, delicious morsels represent the raw ocean incarnate.

In the past decade, a craft oyster trend has swept the East and West coasts. But take a close look and you'll see oysters on menus almost everywhere. From the most highly rated restaurant to the greasy dive down the street, many different places are teasing customers into their establishments with the promise of bliss on the half-shell. You may even see vendors offering up oysters as you're on your Sunday afternoon stroll through town—on the cobblestone streets

of Fells Point in Baltimore, for instance, or in the bustling food fairs in Brooklyn, or along the coastline of Lilliwaup, Washington, and everywhere in between—just as they did in early seaside America.

According to restaurant-industry research by DataSsential, at the end of 2014, oysters appeared on 9.6 percent of all menus nationwide, a 15.7-percent increase from 2010. Fine-dining restaurants saw a 40 percent increase of oysters on their menus. Raw oysters can sell for $3 or more apiece these days. The premium price is not arbitrary. Crafting the oyster is an art. Its form and essence are the work of the watchful eyes and caring hands that raised and harvested it.

This boom of craft oysters is on par with the tidal-wave popularity of other recent food and beverage trends. In the same way that craft beer seeded the idea that microbrews weren't just for experimenting at home, but could appeal to discerning palates at bar taps and in bottles across the nation, crafted oysters have gone from being a specialized coastal or high-end food to appearing on iced trays across the country. Similarly, the wine industry went through the move from commodity to specific branding a few decades ago. More recently, coffee has joined the craft movement and hot sauce has entered the fray.

Kent Messer, a researcher from the University of Delaware, made the comparison with coffee in a three-year study of the oyster industry: "Recall the history of coffee in the U.S. It used to be a commodity—a couple of big companies put coffee into a big blue or red can that contained coffee from all over the world that was mixed together and sold at a low price. Now you have many coffee companies and they will sell you coffee from a specific location. It could be Sumatra, Costa Rica, or even specific farms in Mexico. These coffees are sold at a higher price."

The same thing is happening with oysters. The nutritional and health benefits alone are fantastic; oysters provide a nutrient-packed low-calorie food in a small package. Eating a few oysters every day offers the recommended daily allowances of calcium, copper, iodine, iron, magnesium, manganese, phosphorus, and zinc. Omega-3 fatty acids abound for additional goodness. Foodies have flocked not only to the diversity of oyster types and their associated flavors, but also to the environmental ethos behind their cultivation.

Oysters are extremely sustainable. They don't need additional food sources beyond what's already in the water. All the time they're in the water, they're also cleaning it. They may seem like just two shells with a tasty morsel inside, but they are actually essential cogs in marine aquaculture. Get a load of oysters together, and the reefs they form not only filter water and provide nutrients for a whole host of aquatic life, but they help naturally protect coastlines from storm surges. Talk about a perfect food.

Oyster farmers recognize this high value, but educating the public is a key goal of the industry, both for growth and for future sustainability. The more people know of the benefits of oysters, the more they eat, and the more the industry thrives. As the saying goes, "A rising tide floats all boats." Cheers to that.

Crucially, it's no longer just about the word "oysters" on a menu. Take a glimpse at the offerings on raw bar menus today and you're bound to do a double take at catchy names such as Widow's Hole, Holy Grail, Lady Chatterley, Little Bitches, Wicked Pissah, "Effing" Oysters, Murder Point, and a plethora of other creative and clever monikers. Eaters can now craft their own artisanal half-shell adventure with offerings from around the country. A few years back, it would be common to order a few bland oysters and think nothing of it. An unmemorable experience. An oyster was an oyster. But today's oysters are crafted around a kaleidoscope of flavor, as the subtle notes of the local waters balance the flavorful meats. It's like discovering an ultra-hopped-up IPA beer, an earthy Malbec wine, or a bold, robust coffee. Once you find an oyster that calls out to your taste buds, your senses are awakened and you keep coming back for more.

For a long time, oysters, to me, were just that: oysters. I've always considered myself an adventurous eater and enjoyed oysters on occasion. I knew the basic types of oysters out there—East, West, Gulf—and I knew the general flavor differences between them. But that all changed when I began to discover the phenomenal regional diversity of oysters.

It started with a cross-country trip. After living in New York City for well over a decade, I needed a reset from the daily grind, and I ended up on the road solo for six months, exploring the amazing landscape of the United States. And what I discovered was that coastal cities, towns, and villages offered bivalves from places and with names I've never heard of, often hyperlocal. Eating Norumbegas on the seaweed-strewn seaside in Maine, being mesmerized by the skills of the shuckers at Acme Oyster House in New Orleans, or gazing at foggy San Francisco Bay while downing a dozen (or two) West Coast delights at Hog Island Oyster Company, I was struck by one thing: Everywhere I went, there were phenomenal oysters. Once that shell of interest was opened, it was hard not to dive in.

In talking to servers, shuckers, restaurant owners, and oyster farmers around the country, I not only learned about the intrinsic nuances of flavor that make each oyster distinct, but also the methods used to raise and harvest them, the amazing hard work that the farmers put into them, and their stories. Suddenly, I wanted to know as much as I could about these bivalves—as well as tasting as many as I could!

When I returned to New York City, I began to frequent restaurants that were

oyster-centric to see what new oysters might arrive. Places such as the Grand Central Oyster Bar and the John Dory Oyster Bar were my schools—these eateries went far beyond just carrying an "oyster" on their menu, with lists that were sizable and changed daily.

As I started to pay closer attention, I witnessed the rapid growth and burgeoning popularity of the oyster happy hour. Soon, more venues offering these tasty ocean delights began popping up. Places such as Maison Premiere in Brooklyn and, ultimately, my personal mecca of oysters, Upstate Craft Beer & Oyster Bar in the East Village of New York City were emblematic of this shift. The latter establishment, run by Shane Covey, consistently has 20 to 30 different oysters on the menu, often delivered that same morning by the farmers themselves. There, I spent many a cozy evening chatting with him,

friends, and the farmers who would pop in for a bite and a beverage, discussing the robust world of oysters and oyster farming. Each visit was enlightening, engaging, and enriching.

I learned that oysters were once a staple of American coastal life. At the turn of the century, they could be found everywhere: street vendors, oyster cellars and pubs, home kitchens, you name it. Our ravenous appetite for oysters eventually outpaced supplies, and, further diminished by an onslaught of diseases, their numbers dwindled to the point where wild populations nearly vanished. Compared to the prime oyster-eating era when tens of millions of bushels a year were being consumed, this current American oyster renaissance is still in its infancy. But it is starting to make waves.

Today, oysters are once again a hot item. Or perhaps, better yet, they're cool again. This burgeoning golden era of craft oysters is driven by small, local farms using sustainable farming methods that use only the surrounding environment to grow oysters. They're natural, organic, and truly farm-to-table, or rather, tide-to-table. You're supporting farms that might often have harvested the oysters within a few days of your eating them, if not a few hours. Pure foodie bliss!

With oysters now so accessible to savvy eaters across America, how does someone new to the oyster world know where to begin? And with new oysters hitting the market every year, how does a connoisseur keep up?

PART I

WHY THE *SHUCK* SHOULD I LEARN ABOUT OYSTERS?

"Eating raw oysters is like French kissing the sea. No other food can offer this sort of experience."

—*French poet Leon-Paul Fargue*

Understanding and appreciating oysters is very much like understanding wine. How so? Let's look at the concept of *terroir*, or "a sense of place." Just as different soils impart flavor to the grapes that create wine, different underwater locales infuse their subtle flavor profile into the individual oyster as it feeds. An oyster gets its grub by filtering water through its body, extracting plankton, algae, and other vegetation through small, hair-like cilia as it does so. The food is trapped and then directed into its mouth. As the oyster chows down, it converts all those essential goodies into sugars, fat, and protein that it stores in its body.

This results in a pleasing range of tastes, not only within varieties of oysters, but in a single oyster itself. Brine, sweetness, creaminess, metallics, florals, and fruits can all reveal themselves on the palate within a single taste of an oyster, for those who know what to look for. Since water, not land, is the key ingredient here, the term *merroir* was born, deriving from the Latin word for "sea."

Knowledge is power when it comes to eating, and eating well. Oysters offer not only a delightful sensory experience but also a lot of information in that wonderful shell. The world of oysters is much bigger than you realize; there's nothing better than a sensational mix of a dozen oysters sitting on ice in front of you to start a great conversation. Once your curiosity is piqued about the backstory of the oyster and how it got onto the plate, you become deeply engaged and connected with the food and the people around you. Toss in the intrigue implied by eclectic and esoteric names like Murder Point or Sweet Jesus, and questions will start flying.

Fortunately, once you have a solid foundation of knowledge, oysters aren't overwhelming. In fact, they should never be overwhelming. You always have the option to slurp back a few with a cold one and think nothing of it. But once you have your bases covered, you'll start appreciating and enjoying oysters even more, and you can impress everyone with the amount you've learned. You'll have a story to share, and a delectable one at that.

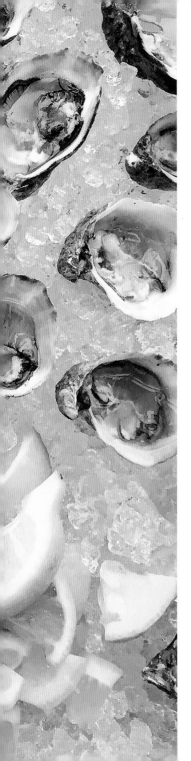

CHAPTER 1

FUNDAMENTALS

"You needn't tell me that a man who doesn't love oysters . . . has got a soul, or a stomach either. He's simply got the instinct for being unhappy."

—*Saki, pen name of Scottish writer Hector Hugh Munro*

Whether you're new to oysters and don't know where you might enter this delectable universe, or you're already well-versed and have your own particular tasting ritual, there are a few simple guidelines to keep in the back of your mind that will lead the way on a fantastic tasting voyage.

The delightful thing about oysters is that, for the most part, you are only committed to eat as many as you wish. You don't have to have oysters as a huge main course that requires a doggy-bag (or fishing net) for leftovers. Oysters can make an enjoyable appetizer, or you can add more to make them your main dish. On many an occasion,

I've found myself out with friends who love oysters, and those who have never tried them, ordering round after round of a dozen old favorites or new discoveries, only to realize that a main course was not on the horizon as we made our way through a bountiful oyster list twice over. You can become so lost in discussions of the nuances of flavor, harvest locations, names, shells, sizes, and other variables that you lose count of how many you've slurped down.

On the opposite end of the spectrum is the lone adventurer, who orders up just one oyster to see what the hype is all about. It won't ruin your appetite for the rest of the menu, and certainly not dessert. In fact, some oysters are wonderful as a cap on a delicious meal. But more often than not, it's impossible to eat just one and not have a few more.

CHOOSING OYSTERS

Depending on the venue and the menu, you may have a few choices of oysters or a few dozen. Choosing which oyster to eat may feel like a daunting task at first, if you don't know what to look for. But take a deep breath. The menu should tell you, at minimum, what region or location the oyster originates from. The oysters might be labeled simply as East Coast and West Coast, or the specific name and origin point of each oyster might be listed. The more detailed the listing, the better the supplier. It usually means the venue's manager or owner took time to source the oysters either through a distributor or the oyster farmer themselves. If nothing is listed, your waiter or shucker should be able to give you the rundown on the varieties they are serving, as well as advice about an oyster before you order. That's what waiters and shuckers are there for.

Which to pick?

A general rule of thumb is that East Coast oysters tend to have more brine and leaner meats, while West Coast oysters tend to be sweeter and creamier with plumper meats. Gulf Coast oysters trend in the middle of those flavor profiles. And sizes can range from petite (around 1½ to 2 inches) to the size of your open hand. (Yes. That big.) However, it is rare to find the largest size on most menus, as the average American oyster eater prefers the 2 to 4 inch range for easy eating. It truly is a matter of preference.

Two are better than one

Beginners should order at least two oysters of the same kind to get a solid sense of how a distinct variety tastes. There will always be subtle variations in an individual oyster type's flavor, so getting at least two will help you form a more complete impression of that taste. You never get a second chance to make a first impression, right?

If you're feeling a little more daring, or if you've tried your first two and were intrigued, a good option is to get several varieties, from all the coasts if possible. A half-dozen is nice. A dozen oysters is an even better place to start. You'll get a fantastic sample of each kind of oyster, picking up the subtle and not-so-subtle differences in nose, body, flavor, and texture.

EATING OYSTERS

The moment when your plate arrives and is being set in front of you, with the oysters glistening on a wispy scent of sea air, is a magical experience. If you ordered more than one type, the server should go over the names of the oysters and where they are on the plate, like this: "Starting at the lemon and moving clockwise. . . ." Different venues have different presentation methods, but one thing common to all good oyster spots is that raw oysters will appear on ice. Crushed ice is best, so the shells can snuggle in and the cup they're sitting in stays upright. It also keeps the oysters nice and chilled, so that you can really take your time to savor their fresh, crisp taste. If they're not on ice, make sure you verify that they have been chilled or have been on ice. At oyster festivals, parties, or events, it's acceptable to grab a few oysters and pop them on a paper plate, or even grab them one at a time, as

long as you're snagging them directly from the ice where they're being shucked or, even better, from the shucker. If you have no idea how long an oyster has been sitting out, eating it isn't worth the risk.

Eat with your eyes

Now that you have some amazing bivalves in front of you, the first thing you'll want to do is to take it all in. Yeah, #foodporn time. Feel free to grab a picture. I'll wait.

Once you've snapped to your heart's content, take a really close look at what you'll be eating. Consider the form of the shells, the meats inside them, and the amount of liquor they hold. Because presentation is as important as flavor, the oyster farmer has worked hard to make their oyster stand out from the others. But usually the last piece of the process is out of the farmer's control: the shucking. A bad shuck can easily ruin an oyster by puncturing the meat, making lots of shell debris, or dumping out the amazing liquor, all of which are tragedies for oyster consumption. Keep an eye open for all of these nuances when that plate of pretty oysters arrives. A fresh oyster will have a good amount of liquor and ample meat. It shouldn't look dry or thin. If it does, it's not very fresh and you shouldn't eat it.

Eat with your nose

Take a whiff and trust your nose. It's on your face for a reason. The human sense of smell is ultra-powerful, even more so than the sense of taste. Ideally, the oyster will have a distinct smell of ocean, greens, or even melons and flowers. Close your eyes and you should be able to imagine yourself on the water's edge. If the oyster smells fishy or funky, don't eat it. Your nose will pick up on all of this right away. Some oysters do have very distinct smells and flavors that may seem off-putting, especially to a novice oyster eater, but the menu, or your server, should point that out. Always ask if you are unsure.

Sip before you slurp

Once you've waved that shell under your nose, take note of the liquor in the shell. With super-fresh oysters, you'll probably notice the liquor first. As you go to smell the oyster, you'll inevitably spill this liquor out on the plate, your hand, the table, or wherever else before its aroma even reaches your nose. Try not to lose it all, and drink it up! The liquor is as important as the substance of the oyster itself. Whether you take a sip of it before eating the oyster, or have it all together, be sure to savor the flavor. The liquor is the water the oyster called home until it was harvested, allowing the oyster to sustain itself for days, if not a couple weeks, under the right conditions once plucked from the water. Pouring the liquor out is a faux pas of the utmost degree. Keep an eye out for this when the oysters arrive. Little or no liquor with an oyster most likely means either that the oysters aren't very fresh or that the shucker isn't up to snuff and has punctured the shell, or *gasp* dumped the liquor out.

Go naked!

Usually, a standard set of condiments accompanies oysters, either on the plate or just off to the side. These include lemon, mignonette, horseradish, Tabasco, and/or cocktail sauce. Some venues riff on variations of these accoutrements, especially the mignonettes, with some fantastic flavor combinations. But for the ultimate tasting experience, purists know that there is no better way to eat an oyster than in all its buck-naked glory. Hold off on the condiments, if you can; you should try at least one of each kind of oyster. This way, you'll get the true flavor of the oyster and can then you can decide how to accent it, if at all.

Once all that savory goodness settles on your palate, you can then figure out what might work best to accompany those hints of brine, melon, cream, and so on. Using a few drops of lemon or mignonette can accent different flavors, while also bringing out new ones within the oyster. The slight acidity from the accoutrements helps queue up your taste buds for other flavors within the oyster as well as balancing the brine. But don't overdo it. That person next to you throwing a giant dollop of cocktail sauce, or heaps of horseradish, onto a delectable oyster is a cringe-worthy sight. Down with cocktail sauce! If you are adding condiments of any kind, don't drown the wonderful flavors of the oyster, just enhance them. It's all about subtlety and balance. I've provided

eclectic palate pairings later in the book that you can try once you get a handle on the basics, but the beauty of an oyster lies in its raw, unfettered flavor.

Nudge away!

You won't need much equipment to eat the oyster, if it's properly shucked. And you already have one readily available, whether you know it or not! Your finger truly is the best tool to guide the oyster into your gullet. You'll most likely also be provided with a cocktail fork if you need it. You can use it to nudge or scoop the oyster if you don't feel like using a digit, but be careful. Make sure to not jab it into the oyster body or damage the meat. Sometimes a bad shuck means that the oyster isn't completely separated from the shell and thus will not slide easily into your mouth. It happens. You may need to slurp a little harder or use the fork to gently complete the separation. You should never stab and chop at the oyster to get it moving out of the shell. And don't even think of slicing up the oyster. They're meant to be eaten whole.

Here's the basic method: Grab the oyster shell on each side with your thumb and index finger, with the hinge end facing or tucked into (depending on the size of the oyster) the soft nook your fingers create. Lift it up, and be careful not to spill any of that delectable fluid. Take a sip, use your finger to wiggle the oyster into a good slurping position, and then tilt the shell up and slide the oyster into your mouth. Let the fun begin.

Chew, don't swallow

The biggest reason not to puncture or slice the oyster into pieces first? Chewing an oyster releases the natural sugars within the delicious meat and greatly enhances the flavor. If you puncture the oyster with a shucking knife, a fork, or something else, all those flavors are released at the same time, and they mix together. Think of it as if you have a delicious meal sitting in front of you, and you decide to mash everything on your plate together before you eat. The flavors may all be there, but the combination lessens the notes of each flavor as it rolls over your tongue. The same goes for swallowing the oyster whole. While chewing reveals a magical symphony of taste, swallowing an oyster whole only allows you a peek at a couple of notes.

Savor that flavor

A common mistake many novice and even some experienced oyster eaters make is either swallowing the oyster whole or taking a few quick bites and calling it a day while swigging from a beverage right after eating, washing away all that amazing aqua-cultured piquancy. After you taste the oyster, take a moment to relish and appreciate what just happened. Initial impressions are so important, and, if it's your first time trying an oyster, or trying a new variety, what you notice first makes a world of difference to your experience. Is the taste comparable to a subtle flavor journey with just hints of salts? Is it like diving into the ocean? Does the earthy flavor jump out at you? Is it all of these things? As you become attuned to the oyster's different kinds of zest, you'll notice how they change throughout. If you rush through this experience, you're missing the best part of eating an oyster. A smack of brine rolling into delicate sugars. Salted vegetals morphing into rich metallics. Wet earth sprinkled under melon tones. All of these subtleties lie in wait for you if you're paying attention.

And the flavor isn't the only thing to savor. The texture is an added bonus. Is it creamy, lean, firm, crunchy, plump, or tender? An oyster sitting in its shell does not give away its texture. A lot can be revealed through a roll around the tongue, both during and through the finish. See what flavors and textures you can discern as you eat,

along with all the subtle nuances that are hanging around for the finish once you swallow.

Leave no liquor behind either! If there is a little puddle of tasty liquid lying at the bottom of the shell once you've slurped your fill, be sure to polish it off. A great bookend to the experience, it will keep your palate primed for the next go-round, especially if it's the same oyster variety. You may pick up on additional different aspects of the oyster's flavor, now that you've tasted your first one.

The Finale

Return the shell to its original spot on the plate to make it easier to identify which kind of oyster you're eating. And, although it's not required, it's fun to flip the oyster upside down back on the plate. Examining the attractive array of shells is a satisfying way to complete

your tasting. When you look at the shells, you can see the similarities and differences in the details of color, shape, and texture. Oyster farmers take great pride in crafting a consistent oyster, both inside and out.

From start to finish, the oyster eating experience is just that: an experience. Referring to these little pointers at the back of your mind while you partake in the wonderful world of oyster eating will keep you engaged and make the journey even more enjoyable.

DISTINGUISHING FLAVORS

Tasting wheels have been popular tools for diners for quite some time. Some wheels are easier to use than others, but they can all help to identify and distinguish the many subtle characteristics and nuances of flavor within a specific food or drink. Oyster eaters may find using a flavor wheel particularly useful as they learn to recognize an oyster's merroir, the taste acquired from its environment, and to help determine the subtle differences between two oysters that may be extremely similar in many ways. Having a tasting wheel as a resource can really put the "Oh, yeah! I taste that!" into an eater's mind, making the eating experience all the more profound.

Nose, body, texture, and finish make up the tasting experience at its core. The pleasure of eating lies in that combination of sight, smell, and taste. As you experience the spectrum of elements in your oyster tasting, take note of each one as you indulge and see what you can pick up.

Taste used to be only four things—salty, sweet, sour, and bitter. These have been long agreed upon. More recently, umami has come to be accepted by modern science as a fifth basic taste, even though the savory flavor has been known in the culinary world for a very long time. There are many more sensations of taste (things like calcium, piquancy, and coolness), but those are more reliant on the sense of smell in combination with taste. That's why, when you have a stuffy nose from a cold, or if you plug your nose, you can only taste the five basics. When your sense of smell is added to the mix, an aroma is

created by flavor changes as you chew. When you're eating, you sense texture and flavor on your tongue and palate, while your nose captures aroma. During the finish, all those elements hang around for a bit longer in your mouth, meld together, and can ultimately be either very different from or extremely similar to your first bite.

Try this fun experiment. When you first put the oyster into your mouth, don't take a bite—unless, of course, it's a bigger oyster. In that case, chomping is a necessity. Let the meat cover your taste buds, and take note of the initial tastes. Novice oyster eaters might be put off by the texture at first, but it's all part of this profound foodie experience.

You'll get the initial zests and, as the oyster warms slightly in your mouth, you'll notice more flavors coming through. As you take your first bite, chew *slowly*, noticing the texture and also how, as the sugars in the oysters are released, the aroma kicks in and changes the flavors.

One of the more amazing attributes of an oyster is that its taste and texture fluctuates as the year progresses. In preparing for winter, an oyster will eat and eat to fatten itself up for hibernation in the cold waters, while in summer, an oyster is getting ready to spawn in the warmer water. The same type of oyster can have a dramatically different flavor profile, depending on the season.

Here are the basics to look for as you taste:

NOSE

The scent can run from a very neutral tone to a mild sea salt odor. You may be able to pick up on even more subtle tones from fragrant florals and simple spices, depending on how keen your sense of smell is.

BODY

This can have a wide range. The term can be used to refer to the visual standpoint (how plump an oyster is), but here it applies to the flavor. Oysters can have a range of tastes, from delicate salts all the way to the taste of subtle fruits and rich vegetation. You may even pick up on hearty earth, wood, and nut flavors.

TEXTURE

This sensation is all about the mouth feel. From thin and watery, crisp and chewy, to plump and pillowy, creamy and silky, these are a few of the textures you may encounter. Sometimes the oyster can surprise you. A few rolls around the tongue as you chew will divulge great secrets.

FINISH

Don't take a drink right after you have an oyster! Pay close attention to how all that wonderful flavor lingers on your palate. It may change subtly or dramatically after chewing. From extremely clean to sweet, earthy, metallic, or even acidic, the way the oyster finishes is almost as fun as that first taste.

Now that you have a good foundation of knowledge, you can challenge yourself to continually enhance your oyster wisdom and gain confidence in both choosing and tasting oysters. You'll impress not only yourself, but friends and family as well.

PAIRING OYSTERS AND DRINKS

Pairing booze and oysters is nothing new. In fact, America has a long history of doing just that. In the early nineteenth century, patrons developed their taste for combining spirits and oysters in bars across the coastal cities. When you think of a high-society party, you may think of oysters and champagne. Today, oysters might have a picture-worthy place next to a tasty craft cocktail of your choice. Depending on the oyster, you'll want to balance the level of brine with the drink. Here are a few general directions to quench your thirst—and you can see the individual oyster listings for specific adventurous pairings.

Wine pairings

Minerality is a nice complement for a lean and briny Atlantic oyster, while a more acidic wine will pair wonderfully with the cream and seagrass notes of a West Coast oyster. White wines fit this bill perfectly, especially if they lean towards the crisp and dry side of the scale. Of course, champagnes and sparkling wines are always a classic.

If I told you that you could eat oysters, drink wine, and help the environment at the same time, you'd do it, right? Well, Berlin Kelly has made it easy. Her company, Proud

Pour, commits to restoring 100 wild oysters to the sea for every bottle of their signature Sauvignon Blanc sold. It's a unique (and boozily tasty) way to bring back the beneficial ecosystem that oysters provide.

Beer pairings

Not too much can beat a cold and crisp lager or pilsner as an oyster partner. For a real treat, the subtle roasted barley caramels of a porter or stout peek through with a briny oyster (think salty-sweet), while a farmhouse ale or saison pairs gratifyingly with the melon-rind hints of a West Coast oyster. IPAs tend to pack a mighty hop wallop that can overpower many oysters, but a lighter session IPA can do the trick. And in the colder months, keep an eye out for some remarkable oyster stouts brewed with real oyster shells.

Spirit pairings

Oyster shooters (similar to a Bloody Mary but with the addition of a raw oyster in the glass) have become trendy in recent years, and the combo can be quite intriguing. The downside is that the high proof of the paired liquor overshadows the oyster. Take it down a notch with something you can sip. A classic dirty martini, gimlet, or even margarita can pair fantastically well with oysters as long as you're not chugging. When sipped, gin and vodka can bring out subtle flavors in the oysters, and vice versa. Sake is an exceptional choice, especially with

West Coast oysters. If you're feeling extremely adventurous, a mezcal, whiskey, or bourbon can kick your tasting experience up a notch.

Absent absinthe?

Quite the contrary. This once-taboo liquor has had a renaissance recently and pairs exquisitely with oysters. Absinthe, however, is an acquired taste for most people, due to its "licorice" essence. An oyster's minerality and brine, when paired with the hints of fennel and mint contained in absinthe, takes on a unique taste sensation that you might either love or hate. If you're looking for something truly unique, this combination is worth a shot.

FUN GAMES TO TEST YOUR OYSTER KNOW-HOW

1 Taste at least a half dozen or a dozen oysters each time you're out to eat. Feel free to keep it to one variety or location or mix it up with a few regions and types. You'll begin to taste the general characteristics of the regions as well as subtle variations associated with each oyster type.

2 Try at least one oyster from each of the five varieties. The more you eat of each variety, the more you'll get to know the attributes of each.

3 A blind taste test is always recommended. By using your other senses (smell, taste), you'll really begin to detect the key flavor points and subtle distinguishing characteristics of the taste of each oyster. Bonus points if you can guess the region. Super bonus high-fives if you can name the oyster!

HOW TO SHUCK AN OYSTER

Get it together

You'll need a decent workspace to start. A flat surface works best.
You should also have a towel on hand to help shuck, clean your knife,
and capture any spillage. Get acquainted with your oyster type's size,
weight, and shape, and keep a bowl of ice on hand to store the
oysters in while you shuck away.

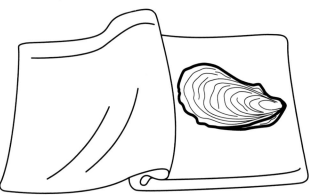

You call that a knife?

You'll need an oyster knife. Not a steak knife. Not a
butter knife. An oyster knife. It doesn't have to be super
fancy one, but it has to be able to get the job done.

Time to get cozy

Nestle the oyster in a towel to keep a good grip on it. You can use a steel-mesh glove to protect your hand as you shuck. Make sure the hinge of the oyster is facing outward and that the oyster is resting on its cup side.

Work the hinge (aka Butt-shucking)

Because this is the tricky part, it takes some practice. Work your oyster knife into the hinge, shimmying back and forth until you get some leverage. You've now reached the sweet spot. Once you've secured leverage, trying to just pry the oyster open will be a fruitless task. Instead, twist the knife like it's a motorcycle handle to get some torque and pop open the shell. You'll feel the shell give once it's ready to open. It may take some work (and possibly Popeye arms), but stick with it. After a few shucks, you'll be an old pro.

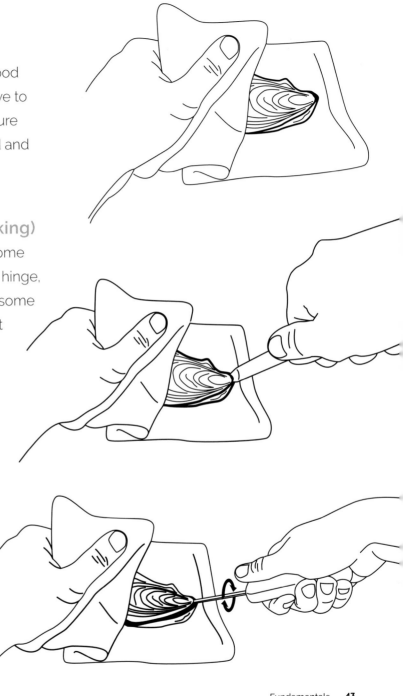

Quick clean

Use your towel to wipe away any mud or silt that may have collected in the hinge after coming off your knife. You don't want dirt getting into your oyster to muck up the flavor.

Sever the adductor muscle

Popping the shell loosens the muscle that holds it shut, but the two halves are still attached. Take your knife and slide the blade across the top inside shell towards the front. You'll feel resistance as you hit the adductor muscle. Slide your knife all the way through and you'll feel the top shell give way, allowing you to remove it.

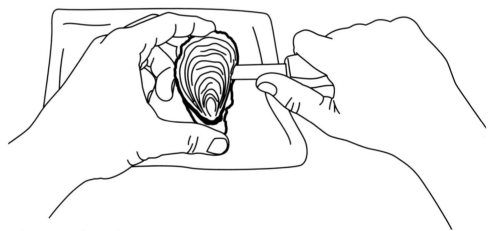

Inspection time

Take a look at the oyster to make sure it looks fresh, with a good amount of liquor. Also take a quick whiff to make sure it smells fresh. Remove any shell fragments that may have gotten into the meat.

Freedom!

The final step is to slide your knife under the bottom of the oyster to dislodge it completely from the adductor muscle. Push your oyster around, if you'd like, to make sure it's completely free. You can flip the oyster over in the shell so it's belly up, which makes for a clean presentation.

Time to plate

You're now ready to put the half shell on ice for serving. Or you can skip this, if you like, and chow down directly! Repeat, on and on.

You must have patience, young shucker. Mastering these steps for a clean and pristine oyster takes some time and practice. As you'll learn, some oysters are easier to shuck than others, so don't be afraid to lose a few in the process. As with anything, though, the more you do it, the easier it becomes.

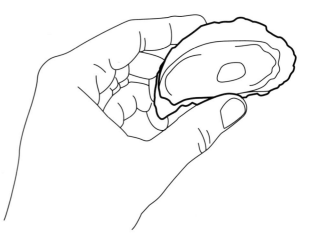

PART II

WHAT DO WE MEAN BY CRAFTING OYSTERS?

"If you don't love life you can't enjoy an oyster; there is a shock of freshness to it and intimations of the ages of man, some piercing intuition of the sea and all its weeds and breezes. [They] shiver you for a split second."

—Eleanor Clark

Farming oysters has become like crafting beer or wine. While the merroir of the aquatic surroundings imbue the oyster with flavor, only the farmer knows where to raise the oyster, and the various methodologies employed in raising it. In the same way that a brew master creates a beer by mixing barley, hops, water, and yeast in various combinations to create different flavors, the oyster farmer has his or her own process for raising delectable oysters. What body of water do you place the oyster in? Where in the water do you place the oyster? What method do you use to raise the oyster? All of these questions, and more, help determine the final features and flavor of the oyster. If you're wondering why some oysters cost so much, the crafting (and care) that goes into raising and harvesting them is the reason.

And, just as in brewing, there are many different scales of production. As with the distance between the small-batch home brewer and the big beer corporation, oyster farming can range from being a tiny undertaking with minimal equipment and personnel to being a large operation with modern methods, up-to-date equipment, and many employees.

It takes a lot of attention for an oyster to get from the water to your plate. Mother Nature may handle the basics, such as water salinity, temperature, nutrients, and tidal flow, but the oyster farmer accounts for and manages these variables as best he or she can to grow the oysters. Bivalves sit around eating the food that's already in the water, filtering microscopic algae (phytoplankton), and absorbing all those delightful flavors coming from the place where they're grown. One of the biggest pluses in raising oysters is that they don't need to feed to create their own protein, unlike a lot of other farmed seafood, such as salmon. It's also why location is so important.

A wild oyster, left to the natural processes of the ocean, will grow in unbounded ways. When growth is unmanaged, shells become long and slender, with thin meats, as each oyster in the reef fights for the best nutrients in the water. Or oysters can grow in another way, and become behemoths as they sit on the ocean floor, taking in as much food they want with no nearby neighbors for competition.

Different farmers have different techniques for raising and harvesting their oysters, but essentially, it boils down to being in the water on a daily basis, seeing how the oysters are growing, and maintaining them until they're ready to harvest. Like great craft brewers, the best oyster farmers have a sixth sense for what works well and what doesn't. Trial and error over the many years they spend growing eventually leads to a consistent quality. That wonderfully smooth shell and uniform cup you see is the result of a process that's been crafted to perfection by the farmer, through knowing the natural methods, or by using the right equipment, or both.

Today, hundreds of oyster varieties are crafted, raised, harvested, and sold in North America. One would think that each variety is its own unique oyster type. But that's not the case. In fact, those hundreds of varieties derive from only five species of oysters. Yup.

Only five. And two of them, the Atlantic and Pacific oyster, are the main drivers. How can that be? Very much like making wine and beer, the watery habitat and the process by which an oyster is raised are the dominant factors that really hone and influence the attributes of the oyster and differentiate it from the others. Hundreds of oyster farms currently exist, and each one is looking for ways to stand out from the rest. And every new oyster farm coming on the market needs to hit upon the right combination of species, location, method, and branding.

This is the crafting of an oyster.

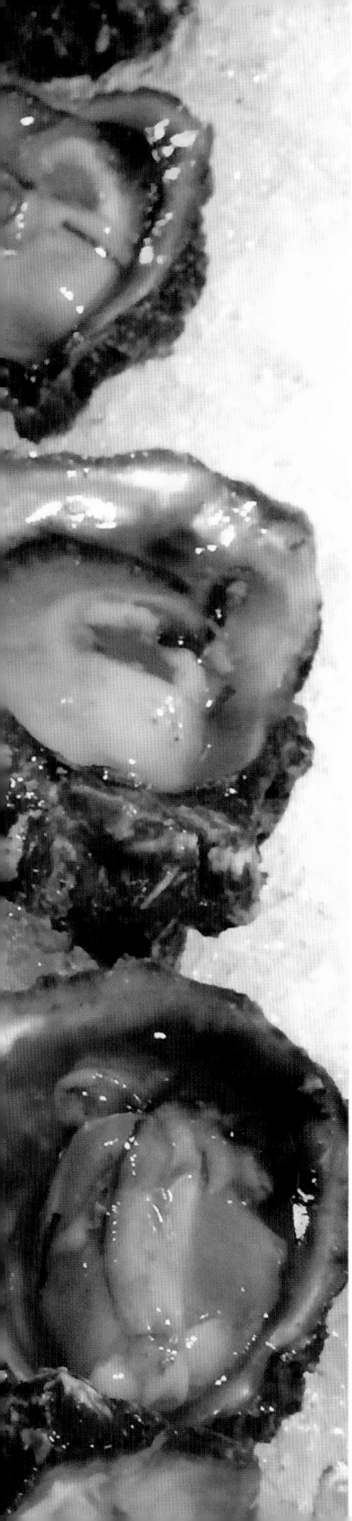

CHAPTER 2

AN OYSTER'S SPECIES

"Why, then the world's mine oyster,

Which I with sword will open."

—*William Shakespeare,* The Merry Wives of Windsor

You've probably seen an oyster's species name on a menu at a fancy restaurant or even at the grocery store in the seafood section. The Latin that resides below the name of the oyster—Crassostrea virginica, Ostrea edulis, etc. would make you think you're at some Roman holiday party. To start, the entire oyster family is called Ostreidae and contains hundreds of oysters. Those you can eat primarily fall under the genera Ostrea, Crassostrea, Ostreola, or Saccostrea. (These are not the oysters you're probably thinking of, the ones that create pearls.) That naming convention is extremely important in letting you know what the flavor foundation is, and what the oyster will end up looking like. These five are the most familiar (and edible) species of oyster that can be found today:

ATLANTIC OYSTERS *(CRASSOSTREA VIRGINICAS)*

Ahh, ye lover of the salt bomb. Rejoice! Virginicas tend to be the briniest of the bunch. And although they're associated mainly with the Northeast, they can be found wrapping their way all along the Atlantic from above the chilly Canadian Maritimes down and around the warmer Gulf of Mexico. In many ways, they're a true American

classic, not least because of their wide availability. Along with the Olympia, they are the only oysters native to North America.

Atlantic oysters are favored by farmers for their vast growing range, their consistent shell shape, and their size. They can have a splendid diversity of proportions and flavors, depending on the water temperatures they grow in. Because cooler waters promote slower growth than warmer waters, Northern Virginicas tend to pack more flavor into a smaller package. But they do tend be the largest of the five species—the average size ranges around 3 to 4 inches at market.

PACIFIC OYSTERS *(CRASSOSTREA GIGAS)*

Considering the Pacific Ocean is the world's largest body of water, it makes sense that the Pacific oyster, then, is the one that's culti-vated the most. According to the National Oceanic and Atmospheric Administration (NOAA), "The Pacific oyster had a worldwide 2010 aquaculture production about seven times larger (by weight) that was worth about 18 times more than production from the Eastern oyster." That's a shelluvah lotta oysters! Strangely enough, they're not indig-enous to the United States or the West Coast. Those titles go to the Eastern and the Olympia oyster. In fact, you will find the Pacific oyster everywhere else in world except on the East and Gulf coasts—and Antarctica.

Because of dwindling Olympia populations from over-harvesting, the Pacific oyster was introduced in North America from its native Japan around the turn of the century to help supplement the native oyster populations. As it turned out, the Pacific oyster loved its new digs on the West Coast, especially in the bountiful and nutrient-rich chilled nooks and crannies of the Northwest, where it spread like wildfire. It helps that the Pacific is a fast-growing oyster. In about 18 months, the Pacifics are ready to head to market.

Compared to Atlantic oysters, Pacifics generally have a sweeter flavor and creamier texture with less brine. It's easy to believe you're tasting melon rind when you bite into some of them. They also have more decorative shell shapes and color than their Atlantic cousins. Their shells often provide an exquisite example of natural growth. Full of rich emerald greens, purples, and grays (amongst others), the shells are rolling, ruffled, and elongated. They truly are works of art.

KUMAMOTO OYSTERS
(CRASSOSTREA SIKAMEA)

Kumamotos are a distinct breed. Literally. They originally fell into the broad Pacific oyster category, which was used to describe any small oyster of that species. However, Kumos, as they're nicknamed, were later found to be a species of their own. The Kumo is also one of the standout names in oysters. If you ask people who are familiar, or even somewhat familiar, with oysters to name a particular type, a Kumamoto is usually what pops to mind. To some, a Kumo is considered the perfect oyster. It's nuanced, yet it's also easily approachable, whether you're a beginner or a knowledgeable connoisseur. Even though they're cultivated in a wide variety of spots on the West Coast, they are known mainly by the name "Kumamoto," with maybe an occasional shout-out to the location, depending on the menu listing.

These oysters originated in their namesake Japanese prefecture of Kumamoto, where, strangely enough, they weren't all that popular. They made the trek over to the United States in the mid-1940s, and, over time, they became a perfect supplement to the Pacific oyster population.

The Kumos make for a great summer treat, as they retain their delicious flavor profile while other oysters are spawning. The Kumo's diminutive size (although it's not as small as an Olympia), bowl-like cup, and gorgeous fluted and colorful shell envelop a delightfully silky smooth textured meat with a creamy, buttery flavor, with hints of minerality and melon on the finish. However, because Kumos take their time to reach a marketable size, they aren't cultivated by many farmers, making them more difficult to find and furthering their status as a top oyster.

BELONS/EUROPEAN FLATS
(OSTREA EDULIS)

Belons are European Flats. But not all European Flats are Belons. Many Flats take on the moniker of Belon for the name value, but Belons are much like Champagne. They can only truly be called Belons if they are plucked near the Belon River in Brittany, Northern France. This makes true Belons a rare breed. They were once hugely popular in Europe, dominating the oyster market there, but over-harvesting, their finicky shell (a weak adductor muscle means these oysters are shipped with a rubber band to keep their shell closed), and their

distinctive flavor, which can be an acquired taste, have made them difficult to find today. The European Flat is having a bit of a renaissance, though, with a few adventurous oyster farms in Washington and Maine starting to raise them.

At first glance, these beautifully flat, emerald-hued, saucer-shaped oysters might look innocent enough. But tucked inside each oyster is a wallop of flavor that only the sincerest of oyster lovers could withstand and adore. Consider the taste something like a 9-volt battery disguised as a lollipop. The distinct, vibrant zinc and seaweed tones are accompanied by a wonderful meaty bite, bordering on crunchy, with a marathon of a finish. This ain't an oyster for the faint of tongue. Nevertheless, it has a grand reputation as a favorite among oyster connoisseurs.

OLYMPIA OYSTERS
(OSTREA LURIDA OR OSTREA CONCHAPHILA)

Even rarer still is this mighty widget of an oyster, the Olympia oyster, also known as "Oly." Olys once abounded up and down the West Coast, an area they called home for millennia. Like the Virginica, they are indigenous to North America, but very different from other North American oysters. Tiny in stature, they make Viriginicas look like behemoths by comparison. They could be considered the perfect mix of the previous four varieties we've looked at here. They tend

to be lean like a Virginica, sweet like a Gigas, and showcase an astounding balance of the metallics that the Belon is known for. All of this comes to you in a package roughly the size of a half-dollar.

Up until the era of the Gold Rush, these oysters were prolific, providing sustenance for people up and down the Pacific seaboard. Their popularity was extraordinary, to a point where they were eaten to the brink of extinction. And, to add insult to injury, industrialization in the early 1900s polluted their waters, destroying what was left of their wild populations. In fact, they were thought to be gone until decades later, when ecologists began finding untouched wild Oly oyster beds tucked away in the waters of Washington's Puget Sound. Unfortunately, only about five percent of Olympia oyster beds remain. This means only a select few oyster farmers in the Pacific Northwest have the distinction of raising and harvesting the Olys for people to enjoy. And they are a real treat.

Efforts are underway to protect and restore the Oly. In collaboration with various community groups, the Puget Sound Restoration Fund (PSRF) has initiated a large-scale restoration project to revitalize native Olympia populations and habitats. The Watershed Project and the Wild Oyster Project in San Francisco, along with the Natural Resources

Conservation Service in Washington State, also continue to work towards rebuilding this magnificent oyster population.

THE OYSTER FOR ALL SEASONS

The X-factor among the oyster species is a particular breed of oyster called the Triploid. Most oysters are Diploids, which spawn in summer. Triploids, however, do not spawn. Yeah, these poor oysters are essentially sterile and can't reproduce. But this means Triploids hold a distinct advantage over the more common Diploid. For one, it means that when regular oysters are becoming thin and watery as they're getting ready to spawn, Triploids stay plump, and they remain full of flavor all throughout the spawning season and into the fall.

The added benefit of not having to use all that energy to spawn and create offspring is that Triploids, overall, grow faster than Diploids. And when you add in the fact that a Diploid can lose up to two-thirds of its body weight after it spawns, that means a Triploid doesn't have to worry about gaining that weight back to get to market size. All of these factors make Triploids quite appealing to some farmers.

CHAPTER 3

OYSTERS IN THE WILD

"An oyster leads a dreadful but exciting life."

—*M. F. K. Fisher*

Since most natural oyster reefs have been depleted at this point, crafting oysters on a farm is now standard. But some wild reefs are still harvested, mainly in areas such as the ACE (the Ashepoo, Combahee, and Edisto rivers) basin in South Carolina near Charleston, and around the Gulf Coast. They make up about 5 percent of the industry. Wild oysters are bottom dwellers, often stuck in the mud, growing in length to fight for the nutrients in the water. These non-farmed oysters don't have the same management or care that a crafted oyster does, so their appearance can be somewhat mangled. Their shells usually grow together, lumping them into a jagged stone-like collective.

The harvester also has a much tougher job collecting them, lumbering through mud flats and chipping away excess shell and dead oysters with a hammer before bringing the good oysters back to be rinsed and cleaned. Often, instead of being served raw, you'll find these oysters served roasted. But some do end up being served on ice.

Wild oysters tend to take their time growing by comparison with crafted oysters, which hit the plate in 12 to 36 months on average. And as these oysters fight the tides without the sanctuary of a bag or cage, the extended time they spend in the water causes them to become somewhat heartier. Their shells become more robust and, subsequently, tougher to shuck, while the meat inside has more room to grow. You can be certain that an oyster crafted by a farmer, who knows the techniques and the waters of their farm better than they know most people, will provide a consistency of flavor and texture head and shoulders above that of an oyster growing wild in the water. Here's an analogy: a wine from your favorite vineyard compared with grape juice that has naturally fermented. Chances are you're going to like what an experienced producer gives you better.

CHAPTER 4

FARMING OYSTERS

"Oysters are the most tender and delicate of all seafoods. They stay in bed all day and night. They never work or take exercise, are stupendous drinkers, and wait for their meals to come to them."

—*Hector Bolitho*, The Glorious Oyster

Oyster crafting takes what wild oysters already have in nature and hones it through methods that fit within an existing habitat. Oyster farmers don't have to clear out fields or buy feed. Compared to wild oysters, crafted oysters have a very cozy lifestyle, growing in cages or bags, safe from any predators around them, and being cared for by the farmer. But it is totally possible that they would sit in the same water and eat the same food as a wild oyster, which would give them extremely similar flavors.

HATCHING THE CRAFT

When oysters spawn, the subsequent cultivation of baby oysters are called "spat". As they grow further, they start to form shells and are called "seed." Whether a farm spawns its own oysters, purchases the seed from hatcheries, or lets the oysters propagate naturally (although this is a riskier proposition for a successful business), they need to have oyster seed to start the crafting process.

Different hatcheries have different processes for cultivating their oyster seed. Lineage plays a big part in the preparation. Good parents mean good offspring, and farmers who create seed are basically playing matchmaker for the bivalves. By picking oysters that have the best traits over many years and breeding them, the farmers create stock that is consistent in shape, size, growth rate, resistance to disease, and many other qualities.

As an eater, you can taste the end result of all the hard work put into crafting an oyster. Keeping a close eye on oysters and maintaining them is one piece of the puzzle. Only a select few farms take the extra starting steps of hatching their own oysters and nurturing them until they can take their spot on the farm. Skip Bennett of Island Creek Oysters in Duxbury, Massachusetts, has a pretty unique process at his farm to begin the crafting process: "We have a hatchery team who grow algae, and spawn our oysters for our next season's crop. They start as tiny specks in the water and grow to be about 2 to 3 inches. Once they are pulled from our hatchery, they are put into an upweller system. The oysters hang out in 'silos' with mesh screens at the bottom. We then pump Duxbury Bay water through these boxes so the oysters have as much access to the algae as possible. At this point, they are too little to go out into the bay, so they need to be protected. Eventually, the oysters are held in mesh bags. We call this the nursery. Finally, they are big enough to be planted. We 'shovel' them off of the boat, where they hang out on the bottom of Duxbury Bay for about another year. It definitely has been trial and error through the years, and [we're] always experimenting with new ways to make it better!" Let's look at the various stages of this process.

GETTING IN THE MOOD

The tricky part is getting the oysters to spawn at the right time. Most oyster planting takes place in the late summer so that the oysters are a large enough size to make it through the winter months. However, summer is usually when oysters like to get frisky and release their goods into the wild. On the other hand, during winter, when the water is colder, oysters are cozily snoozing in their shells, fattened up from eating to get through their slumber. They certainly aren't in the mood to get it on. They ultimately take their cues from the environment around them. A little mood lighting and romantic music, though, doesn't do the trick. So, to get oysters to abide by farming schedules, hatcheries condition their oysters to get them in the mood. Once one oyster starts to spawn, all the rest will follow. By providing a setting full of their favorite food, phytoplankton, and warming up the water around them, it . . . is . . . on. Oh, yeah.

Once fertilized, the eggs are moved to separate tanks. These tanks hold upwards of tens of millions of little ones waiting to grow up. The conditions are well controlled, so that when the microscopic larvae form and are looking for food to eat, they are living in optimal conditions, with water that contains all they need.

These baby oysters are monitored, inspected, and tended to closely for weeks as they continue to develop. After a few weeks, they are primed for their next phase in life, which is to quit swimming around and settle down in a place they can call their own. Normally, in the wild, they'd find something solid to attach themselves to—a rock, a pier, other oysters—and call it a life. In a hatchery, the best material to attach to is provided by old oyster shells. Whether whole or ground up, piles of old shells make a baby oyster's preferred dwelling. After a few weeks of growth, it's time for the baby oysters to leave the cozy comforts of the hatchery and move on to their next destination.

To put this part of the process in perspective, a million baby oysters can fit into two pint glasses and weigh a little over two pounds. By the time they reach adulthood, those same oysters can take up an acre of water real estate and can tip the scales at upwards of a million pounds!

It's a rarity for farms to also run their own hatcheries. In addition to growing oysters from that stock, the seed can be purchased or supplied to other farms. Many oysters you eat could be from the same hatchery, or even the same stock. Those millions of baby oysters shipped to various locations to grow, will take on the distinct flavors, the merroir, of their respective new watery homes.

ENTERING THE LIFE AQUATIC

The oyster nursery is the next stop on the oyster's path to your plate, a perfect environment full of natural nourishment, where they can continue to grow into adulthood. The nurseries can be fine-meshed bags, netted boxes, or other containers, usually with a system in place to provide a huge amount of water flow through the space. Called upweller or downweller systems, they push through a smorgasbord of edible goodness like phytoplankton, algae, and other nutrients for the baby oysters to eat.

Over the next few months, the farmers watch the oysters carefully, monitoring their progress. Because they sprout at different rates, they are constantly sized and sorted to give them all the best chance to survive. This process takes them through their winter hibernation and into the next spring, when they'll be ready to be placed into their final home or sold to other farmers to continue their journey, in a process called growing out.

DIVERSIFICATION

Of the tens of millions of seed that a hatchery can create and raise during this process, a large majority goes to various farms. This is where the final crafting begins. The grow-out method employs the widest range of diversification for the oyster in terms of flavor, texture, and shell shape. This is when the oyster truly grows up. As mentioned earlier, two oysters can be exactly the same in many ways, but the place where each spends its life eating and acquiring its merroir makes it a different varietal. In beer terms, it would be like taking a blonde ale and deciding to cask-age it in an oak barrel for a few months, versus an ale that is wet hopped. Even on the same farm, that identical seed can be split into two different grow-out methods with wonderfully different results.

LOCATION, LOCATION, LOCATION

It's all about where you are. The oyster's individual appeal is largely decided by what's in the water surrounding it, so much so, in fact, that the flavor of an oyster can change hourly, based on things like rain and tidal flow. In fact, many oyster farms can be located within a few hundred yards of each other; the farms optimize their farming and harvesting locations based on this information. Water salinity, temperature, and nutrient flow are vital factors shaping the flavor of an oyster, accounting for much of what the farmer looks for. The technology farmers use ranges from the simple, such as using tumbling machines to shape the shells, to the complex, like engineering phytoplankton for oysters to eat and using 3D mapping of ocean floors to gauge the best locations to place oysters. But at the core of what makes each crafted oyster so flavorful lie the years of experimentation. Like a craft brewer, who often tinkers with different yeasts, blends of hops, and other ingredients (oyster stout anyone?), the oyster farmer learns from the waters he or she harvests in and crafts bivalves with the same tender love and care that a master brewer uses.

METHODOLOGY

Farmers use a variety of methods to grow their oysters. From rack-and-bag to beach conditioning, each technique produces a different result. Farmers may incorporate one or multiple procedures to grow their oysters.

Things get interesting when a farmer combines or adjusts techniques within the growing of one oyster type, creating contrasting varieties. One oyster might be submerged in a cage at the edge of the ocean, where it fights tides to become a briny, smooth, lean oyster, while its neighbor might sit in an off-bottom bag, comfortably floating in a nutrient-rich current, getting plump and curvaceous.

CAGE

Cages are secured by their bottoms in a manner that keeps them out of the mud and silt and prevents them from floating away. Growers tend to use younger oysters for this method, to provide lots of water flow and protection from predators such as fish, birds, crabs, otters, and rays.

TUMBLING

This technique helps eliminate excess shell from the oyster. A farmer runs the oysters through a motorized barrel that flips them over and over (like a run through the funhouse), breaking up excess shell growth around the edges of the oyster. Tumbling forces the shell to grow deeper and smoother, creating those wonderful cup shapes. It also helps strengthen the adductor muscle, which keeps the shell closed and creates firmer meats. Think of it as CrossFit for an oyster. The more intense the workout, the leaner, firmer, and stronger they get.

This method is labor intensive, not only for the oyster, but for the farmer. The farmer has to get the oysters out of their bags or cages, put them through the tumbler, collect them, and then place them back in their container and return them to the water. A simpler version of the process takes advantage of natural wave patterns and tidal flows while the oysters are still in their bags or cages. Strung together and tied to floats, the bags rise and fall with the tides, creating a subtle roll and naturally tumbling them. This is a perfect low-maintenance, energy-friendly way to take advantage of this method.

Oysters that aren't tumbled tend to grow long and skinny as they add new layers of shell growth. Like harvest location, the use of the tumbling method can be a big selling point for an oyster.

SURFACE OR FLOATING

The oysters float in mesh bags or cages on or near the surface of the water. Bouncing up and down on the waves provides natural tumbling action. This helps to create cleaner and stronger shells.

BOTTOM OR BEACH

These oysters call the beach home, because that is where they are kept. But their life isn't quite beachy keen. This method makes the oysters work to keep their shells closed, as they're fighting the tidal flows and trying to stay safe against predators.

RACK & BAG

Oysters are anchored slightly in the water column off the sea floor in mesh bags or cages. Since the oysters need to be managed and accessed, the success of this method is highly dependent on the tides in that location. Oysters grown this way have an easier lifestyle; a steady flow of food-rich water and a general lack of predators allows them to grow quickly.

LONGLINE

Oyster seed is attached and suspended from long ropes into the water. Since all the oysters have to hang on to is the rope, they get a good workout as they fight the tides and are exposed to predation. As a result of this rigor, they end up with stronger shells and firmer meats.

SUSPENDED TRAY

Talk about living the pampered life. These oysters get to lounge around in trays in the water, eating their shells off—not literally, but close enough to plump up nice and big. Trays have the advantage of being stackable, to optimize space in the water. Tidal action has a good effect on suspended nets and trays. As the tide rises and falls, so do the oysters. This natural tumbling action of the waves helps give the oyster a workout, which provides a good shell shape and firmer meat.

BAG TO BEACH

This method takes the oysters who are enjoying the good life in the rack and bag method and thrusts them into the sands of the beach environment for the last few months until harvest. Here they can fight the tides, strengthen their shells, and firm up their meat.

What practice makes the most sense for a farmer to use? That's just it. There isn't one true technique that crafts them all. In fact, many crafters do experiment, and, through trial and error, they ultimately find a technique that works best for their specific environment. The result of this technique should bring joy to you, the oyster eater. The more farmers refine their crafting techniques and figure out what works best, the better crafted oysters make it to the market for you to enjoy. You never know what new system is around the corner that will create a knock-your-socks-off oyster.

Abigail Carroll of Nonesuch Oysters uses a mixed crafting method to create two different oysters on her farm, located on the majestic coast of Scarborough, Maine. "We discovered ground seeding by accident. A friend dove to the site and emerged with incredible green oysters that had escaped from our gear and didn't look anything like what we were growing. I instantly fell in love with these oysters and began to ground seed. We still grow some in gear because it's nice to be able to show how sensitive oysters are to their environment. We have very different oysters when we raise them in gear and when we set them free on the bottom. Oysters on the bottom are brinier with a meatier meat. Oysters from gear are more delicate and subtle." The bottom-crafted oysters go by Nonesuch while her gear-crafted oysters are called Abigail Pearls.

Mica Verbrugge of Effingham Oysters takes a different approach. Being located in a phenomenal natural fjord in British Columbia has its advantages for crafting. Mica is able to move his gear based on water conditions to make sure that his oysters are soaking up the best nutrients and are at the perfect temperature.

"Our oysters are finished at 20 feet deep in the winter and 60 feet deep in the summer. Being able to change the depth, the oyster is always in clean cold water. The oyster thinks it's winter, and the fats turn to sugars, making it firm and sweet. But the real secret is that, because they are suspended, they taste like the ocean, not like the beach," Verbrugge says. "When it comes time to harvest, we pull the oysters up, give them a good wash, and load them in the boat. The oysters are iced within 20 minutes of coming out of the water. The secret to a nice oyster is get them out, loaded, and cold fast." Which brings us to harvesting.

HARVEST AND DELIVERY

Orders are fulfilled as needed by the farmers and their crews as they harvest, size, sort, clean, count, and then pack oysters in insulated boxes for shipping—all by hand. Farmers put the tagged bags of oysters in refrigerated trucks for local shipments to restaurants. For further distances, shipments are sent overnight or by next-day delivery. The wonders of modern delivery services means you're getting extremely fresh oysters to your plate, in many cases within 24 to 48 hours of harvest, and even sooner with local deliveries. This is tide-to-table at its finest. The only thing better is sitting in the water and harvesting the oyster yourself.

Farmers are looking to get their product to market, on average, in anywhere from 18 to 36 months. A lot depends on the species of oyster and the location, but a well-fed and well-maintained oyster is going to make it to market much quicker than one that has little oversight. With a farmer's watchful eye during this time period, an oyster can be shaken every day to prevent the shells from growing together; tumbled every week to chip away excess shell growth, as well as strengthen and deepen the shell; and checked for any predators that may want to eat the oyster before you do. And once the harvesting begins, an oyster might not make the cut to go to market and will be tossed back to the water to continue the process and try again another day. It may even be a couple cycles before an oyster is finally on its way to your plate and into your belly.

The time all of this takes is one of the underlying reasons why oysters can be so expensive. The craft really sets a cultivated oyster apart from a wild oyster or other shellfish.

CHAPTER 5

OYSTERS AND THE ENVIRONMENT

"Throughout the nineteenth century, more and more was learned about oysters so that man's proclivity for destroying them was countered by the ability to create them. Such newfound powers were making humankind giddy with science's magical ability to withstand its own foolish excess."

—*Mark Kurlansky*, The Big Oyster

There are some things you can feel good about. There are other things you can feel giddy and beyond ecstatic about. Eating oysters is one of those things. Why? Because oysters are extremely environmentally friendly and sustainable.

But there is a difference between eating wild oysters and eating farmed oysters. According to The Nature Conservancy, more than 85 percent of the world's wild oyster reefs have been lost to the increased acidification of ocean waters caused by climate change, as well as by other factors such as invasive species and farm runoff from the Midwest into the Gulf of Mexico: a scary thought. But with modern aquaculture and shellfish farming methods, almost all of these remaining oyster reefs can be left undisturbed. Oyster reefs have an enormous impact on the environment around them and provide for the foundation of a healthy ecosystem. This makes oysters a keystone species. Yes, it is still possible to harvest and eat wild oysters, but even those are monitored to prevent depleting the populations further.

Climate change is a deep concern for many growers. Subtle changes in water temperature and acidification have a significant impact on the quality of the oyster, also affecting shell growth. There is a glimmer of hope, though. One of the ingredients that shellfish extract from the ocean to manufacture their shells is CO_2. A Woods Hole Oceanographic Institute study in 2009 found that "some shellfish actually thrive in higher CO_2 environments. Oysters make relatively McMansion-sized homes for themselves, compared to other shellfish, making them a good contender for carbon sequestration. Time will tell though, as this is only a possibility in the near future. Too much carbon in the oceans and it actually means oysters would struggle to make a shell."

Oysters, unlike other members of seafood aquaculture, and farmed wildlife in general, don't need to be fed by sources other than the water they're in. Thus, they don't drain and strain resources; instead, they soak up everything they need to grow and live by filtering water around them. And the more nutrients and minerals in the water around them, the faster they'll grow (and the tastier they'll be)! This filtering benefits the surrounding waters, providing a dynamic home for diverse aquatic life. The more oysters there are, the healthier the environment around them becomes.

At one point in the history of New York City, the oyster population was so massive it was capable of filtering all of the water in the harbor in a matter of days. Days! Today, the Billion Oyster Project in NYC is attempting to replicate that historical moment by seeding the Hudson, with the hopes that the oyster will become, once again, a natural filter. Meanwhile, the Oyster Recovery Partnership is doing the same for the Chesapeake Bay after the near collapse of the oyster ecosystem almost 50 years ago from over-harvesting and pollution. Oysters played a critical part in maintaining water quality and providing a cornerstone for marine habitats in both locations. And the interest in these initiatives is palpable. Both the Billion Oyster Project and the Oyster Recovery Partnership network with hundreds of local restaurants for shell recycling programs, collecting hundreds of thousands of shells to use to reestablish and grow the ecosystems. There's nothing better for a new oyster to grow on than an old oyster shell.

"As oyster farmers, we have the privilege of working on the water and contributing to our coastal community," says Tal Petty, owner of the Hollywood Oyster Company, a farm on the Patuxent River in Maryland. "We are constantly amazed by the biodiversity that acres of oyster cages in a 'moving reef' attracts. We get pleasure knowing that we are contributing to the restoration of our watershed by observing the increased animal and plant life around our operations."

For Lissa James Monberg, who is the fifth-generation owner of Hama Hama Oysters on Washington's Olympic Peninsula, it's the larger endeavor that really hits home. "Growing oysters is humbling . . . and it's definitely a social endeavor. We can't just fence off our farm and call it our organic farm. We have to ensure the water coming in with every high tide is clean, and to do that we need to involve lots of other people. We have to work with our neighbors, with our community, with our region, in order to ensure the water quality is good enough to grow filter feeders for food. That's scary, but it's also awesome: this is truly a green industry. Our economics depend on environmental health, and I'm really honored to work in it."

So you can feel fantastic about eating oysters. And then you can enjoy more oysters and feel even more fantastic.

CHAPTER 6

BRANDING OYSTERS

"Man seems born to consume 'oysters.'"

—*Charles Mackay*, Life and Liberty in America, 1857

It's hard to ignore how dominant branding and marketing have become in the oyster industry. Promotion through the internet and social media is very important if you want to get a brand noticed. Nowadays, savvy foodies are just a few finger taps away from a Google search that can reveal a wealth, or severe lack, of information. Eaters are always hungry for more knowledge, and a company name can be an eye-catching tool for grabbing eyes and appetites.

In the late 1800s, the natural habitat for oysters ranged far and wide across the Eastern seaboard, especially in the area around Long Island called the Great South Bay, which was the home of the Blue Point Oyster. In those days, and well into the next century, in coastal cities like New York, oysters were a cheap, easy, and abundant source of protein. They were even more popular than beef! In their abundance, they were most often sold as generic "oysters," but the moniker of Blue Point stood out. You could ask for a Blue Point and know what you were getting. This recognition helped them sell like hotcakes and become a go-to brand. As a result, many oyster farmers at the time began raising inferior oysters under the same tag to ride the coattails of the success of true Blue Points. To maintain some semblance of control over this trend, the New York Legislature in 1903 passed a law that stated, "No person shall sell or offer for sale, any oysters, or label or brand any packages containing oysters for shipment or sale under the name of Blue Point Oysters, other than oysters which have been planted and cultivated at least three months in the waters of Great South Bay." That law is still in place today.

In the 1940s and '50s, Shelter Island Oyster Co. introduced Oscar the Oyster as their brand ambassador. He made his way into print, radio jingles, and other paraphernalia touting the best oysters on the east end of Long Island, New York. This was a step towards capturing a larger audience in the marketplace. Sadly, not many people remember Oscar.

Today, following in Oscar the Oyster's footsteps, farmers are looking for ways to differentiate their oysters within the marketplace and make their brand memorable for the consumer. As more and more locations contain multiple oyster farms within swimming distance of each other, it's become mandatory to set yourself apart if your oyster name isn't already established. How can you distinguish one excellent oyster from another fantastic one? By a catchy name.

That name, in turn, generates interest, not only from restaurants who are looking for items to stand out on their menu, but also for the consumer. How many times have you tried something just because it had a clever or funny name? It's very much like naming a beer. Something eclectic, funny, kitschy, and memorable will garner a lot more interest than just the word "oyster" on a menu. These names can be extremely effective tools, especially considering that most people have a hard time telling the difference between oysters of a similar region or location, say a Malpeque and a Wellfleet. But they'll remember a Puffer's Petite, Fat Dog, Wicked Pissah, Naked Cowboy, or Sweet Jesus. This is where creative names come into play. When people recognize and remember the name of an oyster when they're out or talking about the experience with friends, it helps make that oyster (and all oysters) popular.

So how do oyster farmers choose a name? If they're lucky, the location just happens to carry the perfect note of intrigue. Lane Zirlott's Alabama farm, for example, is near a spot where two oystermen are said to have had a homicidal dispute over the lease on the waters. His Murder Point oysters have a killer name and a catchy tagline: "Oysters worth killing for."

Many oyster names come from their harvest location, meaning they have been long taken by those farms that managed to establish themselves early on in the oyster craze, such as Wellfleet, Duxbury, Hood Canal, or Gulf. If you were a newer oyster farmer producing harvests in these same regions, you'd have had to use some elbow grease and clear some space for yourself. Farmers would look to specific locations to start their farms and then name their oysters after them, as with Widow's Hole, Island Creek, Fanny Bay, or Hama Hama. Some regions and locations might have a fellow oyster farm as close as a few hundred yards away. Many farms today may be raising their oysters from the same oyster seed as their neighbor, with a similar methodology.

But is there a drawback to naming the oyster to stand out from the reef? While there is a certain value in a catchy name, is the origin of the oyster becoming lost on consumers? As the names become funnier and more clever as, in some cases, they push the envelope of good taste with sexual innuendo, the worry is that people will lose the sense of what the harvest location means for that particular oyster. Rather, they'll only remember that they slurped down a funny insider-baseball dad joke or quirky riff on a celebrity name instead.

This debate will continue in the oyster industry, as the popularity of oysters continues to skyrocket and shows no signs of slowing down. Therein lies the dilemma. It can feel as if an effort towards consumer education is diminished when a funny or quirky name is used rather than a regional or local association. But on the other hand, those memorable names have proven to provide a hook for the consumer, and for the chefs and restaurants that buy them. Memorable names also provide a level of accountability, as now an oyster eater will remember the name associated with the quality of that oyster. If a crafted oyster's quality varies wildly from experience to experience, a consumer will take note. Knowing that if a Kumamoto isn't consistent with what you now have set in your mind as a Kumamoto, it will be a disappointment. If it continues to happen, you may find another favorite oyster. That's the kicker: A catchy name can work wonderfully for you or against you. Once people eat an oyster with a catchy name that is flavorless and silty with a brittle shell, they will remember *not* to go back to that particular bivalve.

A few farms have elevated their branding to a whole new level. Hog Island Oyster Company, Hama Hama Oysters, and Island Creek Oyster Company are examples of companies taking the craft entirely from tide-to-table. They raise, harvest, sell direct, and have their own locations that serve their oysters, as well as giving tours. Touring an oyster farm can be a highly enjoyable foodie experience, and is an essential part of oyster education. It's hard to beat being out on the water, plucking a fresh oyster from its habitat, shucking one, slurping it down, and tossing the shell back into the deep, all while learning about the many elements that go into crafting such an amazing edible. It's aquaculture's version of the brewery tour, but with an environmental twist.

At the end of the day, quality is, and should be, the most important factor in the way an oyster is remembered by the eater. And oyster farmers are particularly keen and adept at crafting the best possible oyster they can. It's not only a matter of fact; it's a matter of pride, especially with an industry that has a deep connection to the environment around it. What is in the shell helps sustain this industry. A well-crafted oyster does more than taste scrumptious. It teaches you something.

PART III

85 SHUCKULENT OYSTERS TO SLURP

"The first man gets the oyster, the second man gets the shell."

—*Andrew Carnegie*

THE OYSTERS

38° North
Abigail Pearl
ACE Blade
Bald Point
Barnstable
Beausoleil
Belon
Black Bear
Black Duck Salt
Blackfish Creek
Blue Point
Blue Pool
Breachway
Cape May Salt
Capital

Chatham
Chelsea Gem
Chincoteague
Choptank Sweet
Church Point
Copps Island
Cotuit
Cup Cake
Daisy Bay
Dune Shadow
Eagle Rock
Effingham Inlet
Fanny Bay
Fat Dog
Fiddler's Cove

Fishers Island
Flapjack Point
Forty North Rose Cove
Gold Creek
Hama Hama
Harstine Island
Hog Neck Bay
Hollywood
Holy Grail
Hood Canal
Irish Point
Island Creek
Kumamoto
Kusshi
Lady Chatterley

Little Bitches
Little Island
Louisiana
Malpeque
Moon Rise
Moonstone
Murder Point
Nauti Pilgrim
Nisqually Sweet
Nonesuch
Olympia
Osterville
Oysterponds
Paine's Creek
Paradise

Pemaquid
Pickering Pass
Plymouth Rock
Point aux Pins
Puffer's Petite
Quonnie Rock
Race Point
Riptide
Royal Miyagi
Salt Nugget
Shibumi
Shigoku
Ship Shoal
Stingray
Sun Hollow

Sunken Meadow Gem
Sweet Jesus
Totten Inlet Virginica
Totten Pacific
Wellfleet
Whitecap
Wicked Pissah
Widow's Hole
Wildcat Cove
Wolf Beach

38° North

CRASSOSTREA VIRGINICA

MERROIR A subtle honeyed scent tingles the nose. The delightfully multi-colored shell cradles pristine golden-hued meat. The liquor is plentiful and crisp, with brine and subtle hints of sugar. The lean meat has a gratifying bite with a well-balanced savory flavor. Pockets of earthiness are intermingled with a dash of lemongrass. The finish is perfectly airy with a delicate holdover of brine.

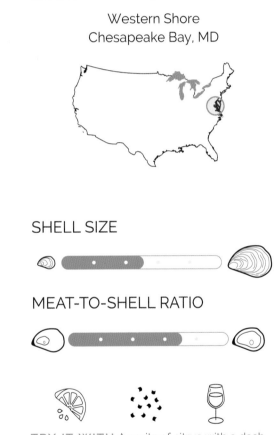

Western Shore
Chesapeake Bay, MD

TASTING PROFILE

BRINE

SWEETNESS

MINERALITY

NOSE

FINISH

TEXTURE

- ✓ LEAN
- ✓ TENDER
- ✓ SILKY
- ✓ SMOOTH

SHELL SIZE

MEAT-TO-SHELL RATIO

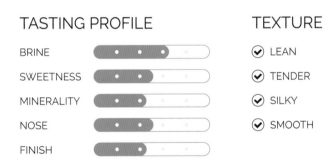

PEARL OF WISDOM 38° North is the geographical location of a series of farms along the banks of Maryland's Western Shore, the southernmost tip of Maryland, where the Chesapeake Bay and Potomac River meet in a picturesque kaleidoscope of sea and natural wetlands.

TRY IT WITH A spritz of citrus with a dash of red pepper flakes. Pair with a simple oaky Chardonnay.

Abigail Pearl

CRASSOSTREA VIRGINICA

MERROIR Wonderful ivory teardrop shape shell with blonde and caramel colors swirled throughout. The faint aroma of salted vegetables hangs over a delectable briny liquor. The golden beige meat sits comfortably in the mouth and stomach. An eye-opening burst of brine lies beneath a tender bite, followed by the succulent sweetness of sautéed snap peas. A pinch of salt grabs the tongue and transitions into fading sugars.

Nonesuch Point
Scarborough, ME

TASTING PROFILE

BRINE

SWEETNESS

MINERALITY

NOSE

FINISH

TEXTURE

- ✓ TENDER
- ✓ TOOTHSOME
- ✓ VELVETY
- ✓ BUTTERY
- ✓ SMOOTH

SHELL SIZE

MEAT-TO-SHELL RATIO

PEARL OF WISDOM This oyster's farmer, Abigail Carroll, has a motto: "Less is more. Nature works well when you let it."

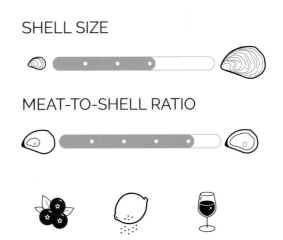

TRY IT WITH A few dried wild Maine blueberries with some lemon zest. Match with a local Maine wild blueberry wine for a divine pairing.

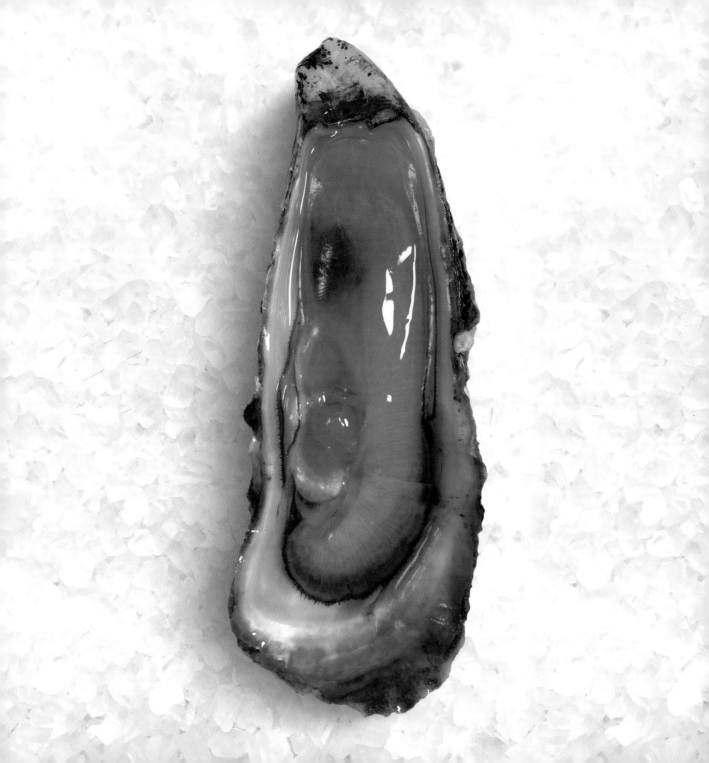

ACE Blade

CRASSOSTREA VIRGINICA

MERROIR The scent is reminiscent of a salty morning breeze over marshland. The slender, vibrant green shell is a deep ravine that houses a lean, golden meat bathing in liquor. Take a sip and be wowed by the super zing of salts. The meat is light and makes for very smooth eating with hints of grass and green pepper. A crisp, clean finish remains for just the right amount of time.

ACE Basin, SC

TASTING PROFILE

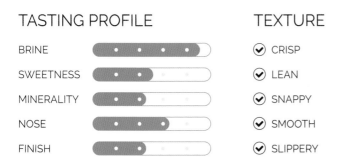

BRINE	
SWEETNESS	
MINERALITY	
NOSE	
FINISH	

TEXTURE

- ✓ CRISP
- ✓ LEAN
- ✓ SNAPPY
- ✓ SMOOTH
- ✓ SLIPPERY

SHELL SIZE

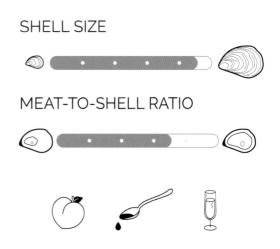

MEAT-TO-SHELL RATIO

PEARL OF WISDOM The ACE Basin, in the South Carolina Lowcountry, spans approximately 350,000 acres and is one of the largest undeveloped estuaries on the Atlantic Coast. It lies at the point where the Ashepoo, Combahee, and Edisto Rivers meet and flow into the larger St. Helena Sound.

TRY IT WITH A simple peach mignonette. Pair with a classic peach Bellini.

Bald Point

CRASSOSTREA GIGAS

MERROIR A scraggly, rippled shell releases an aroma filled with melon and floral notes. The pale, dark-edged meat, albeit on the small size, is portly and tucked into a cozy nook amidst a bright and flavorful liquor. The bite is hearty with a silky texture and a mild brine beginning that transitions into a fruity sweetness. That flavor holds through the finish with hints of muskiness peeking onto the palate.

Hood Canal, WA

TASTING PROFILE

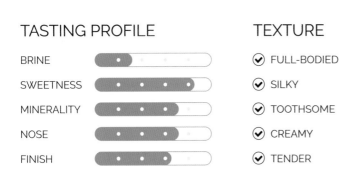

BRINE

SWEETNESS

MINERALITY

NOSE

FINISH

TEXTURE

✓ FULL-BODIED

✓ SILKY

✓ TOOTHSOME

✓ CREAMY

✓ TENDER

SHELL SIZE

MEAT-TO-SHELL RATIO

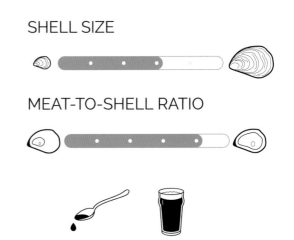

PEARL OF WISDOM The unique features of the Hood Canal—depth and steepness—make it a wonderland for oysters. The cold, deep waters are fed by the surrounding rivers, which have helped to make it a haven of nutrients and minerals that the oysters love, and that provides a flavor distinct to the area.

TRY IT WITH A spoonful of ginger scallion sauce. Best accompanied by a chocolate-tinged porter.

Barnstable

CRASSOSTREA VIRGINICA

MERROIR The yin and yang coloring of the top and bottom near-perfect teardrop-shaped shell is a visual delight only outshone by the stunningly pristine meat. The pure ivory color is drenched in a luscious, briny liquor, tinged with an earthy spinach sweetness from soaking in algae-rich water. The nose is crisp. The texture is quite firm with a wonderful "crunch" that releases subtle hints of nuttiness and sugars laced with brine. Salts roll through the finish with a gentle creaminess.

Barnstable Harbor
Cape Cod, MA

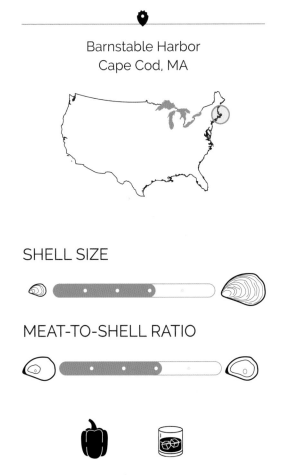

TASTING PROFILE

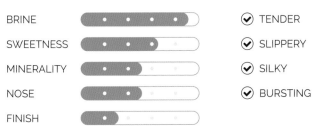

BRINE

SWEETNESS

MINERALITY

NOSE

FINISH

TEXTURE

- ✓ TENDER
- ✓ SLIPPERY
- ✓ SILKY
- ✓ BURSTING

SHELL SIZE

MEAT-TO-SHELL RATIO

PEARL OF WISDOM Although there is the classic "Barnstable" oyster, the name can also refer to any oyster from Barnstable Harbor in the Cape Cod region. This extraordinary location for growing bivalves is also home to Barnstable derivatives including Moon Shoals, Spring Creeks, and Beach Point.

TRY IT WITH A finely diced green pepper for a splendid accent. As a daring liquor pairing, sip a Chartreuse, to unlock even more potential.

Beausoleil

CRASSOSTREA VIRGINICA

MERROIR Beautiful ivory shell tiered with caramel color like tiramisu. The nose is tinged with a wonderfully delicate aroma of simple syrup through a sea mist. The plump meat is firm and packs the shell along with ample briny liquor. A lean texture rolls with flavor, reminiscent of a pat of salted butter on warm, doughy bread. The finish is smooth with hints of tin and a lingering wisp of greens. A very nice starter oyster.

Miramichi Bay
New Brunswick, Canada

TASTING PROFILE

BRINE

SWEETNESS

MINERALITY

NOSE

FINISH

TEXTURE

⊘ SILKY

⊘ BUTTERY

⊘ SMOOTH

⊘ FIRM

SHELL SIZE

MEAT-TO-SHELL RATIO

PEARL OF WISDOM Beausoleils live in the very northern coastal waters of the cold Canadian Atlantic. Although small in stature, around 2 to 3 inches, it still takes around four years for these oysters to reach market size. Patience is well rewarded.

TRY IT WITH A sprinkle orange zest on top to balance the brine. A Lambic beer is an amiable partner.

Belon

OSTREA EDULIS

MERROIR This flat or "plate" oyster has a craggy, round, shallow shell that looks innocuous enough. It starts with a delicate aroma of lettuce. The meat is large and richly colored with a nice firm texture. The liquor has a sweet vegetal flavor. Then, wait for it, a tsunami tornado of a 9-volt zinc battery explosion rushes over the palate and lingers, lingers, lingers. Whether you love it or hate it, you won't find another oyster like this one.

Various Locations
ME, RI, Canada

TASTING PROFILE

BRINE	▓▓▓▓▓░░░
SWEETNESS	▓▓▓░░░░░
MINERALITY	▓▓▓▓▓▓▓
NOSE	▓▓▓░░░░
FINISH	▓▓▓▓▓▓▓

TEXTURE

- ✓ FIRM
- ✓ DENSE
- ✓ MEATY
- ✓ ZINGY
- ✓ LAYERED

SHELL SIZE

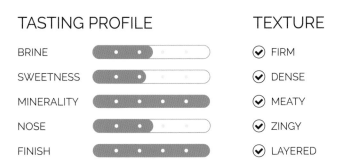

MEAT-TO-SHELL RATIO

PEARL OF WISDOM Belons are the rarest oysters in North America and typically are known as European Flats. The namesake river in France is where the finest Belons originate. They are also cousins of the Pacific Northwest's Olympia oyster, but they belong to an entirely different genus than all other oysters.

TRY IT WITH Nothing. You can't hold a citrus to this one. Or a mignonette for that matter. Even a paired beverage is a faux pas. Enjoy this one in all its scrumptious glory.

Black Bear

CRASSOSTREA VIRGINICA

MERROIR A shallow shell holds a sweet nose of seaweed and rolling river water. The meat is lean and very photogenic, with dark cilia for water filtering. The metallic flavor with big brine notes really comes through in both the liquor and the meat. The finish is crisp and dry with subtle brassy elements.

Bagaduce River, ME

TASTING PROFILE

BRINE	●●●●
SWEETNESS	●●●
MINERALITY	●●
NOSE	●●
FINISH	●

TEXTURE

- ✔ CRISP
- ✔ SLIPPERY
- ✔ SILKY
- ✔ BURSTING
- ✔ CLEAN

SHELL SIZE

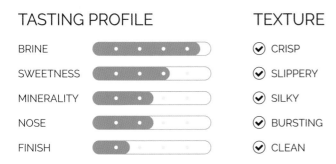

MEAT-TO-SHELL RATIO

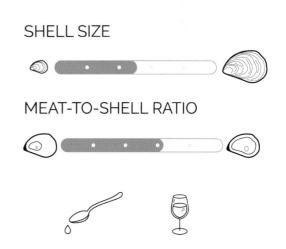

PEARL OF WISDOM Maine's unique coastline, formed by the retreating glaciers of the last Ice Age, is lined with a multitude of long, winding estuaries. Add in the powerful tidal action and the year-round cold waters and you have an ideal location for oysters to prosper.

TRY IT WITH A honey-citrus mignonette and pair with a dry mead. Bears love honey.

Black Duck Salt

CRASSOSTREA VIRGINICA

MERROIR Sporting a chubby shell with classic coloring, these hefty hunks have a peachy meat that's silky smooth with a delectable vegetable broth flavor—Mirepoix style. A hefty but not overpowering brine complements the entire morsel. The finish is smooth; a taste of salted veggies lightly lingers.

Hog Island Bay, VA

TASTING PROFILE

BRINE	●●●
SWEETNESS	●●●●
MINERALITY	●
NOSE	●●
FINISH	●●

TEXTURE

- ✓ SILKY
- ✓ SMOOTH
- ✓ LAYERED
- ✓ SNAPPY
- ✓ BURSTING

SHELL SIZE

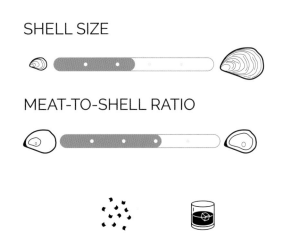

MEAT-TO-SHELL RATIO

PEARL OF WISDOM The Chesapeake Bay region has a rich history of harvesting and eating oysters. The earliest evidence suggests this started as early as 2500 B.C. from the shell deposits in the area, also known as middens.

TRY IT WITH A few bacon bits over the top. To drink, try an Old Fashioned.

Blackfish Creek

CRASSOSTREA VIRGINICA

MERROIR Rich colors of charcoal and bronze flow through the robust shell. The scent of this oyster is reminiscent of walking into a garden after a fresh rain. A quick sip of the liquor is refreshing with a gentle zing of brine. Hints of seagrass and silt with a sublime cucumber sweetness tickle the taste buds. Very meaty with a good chew, this oyster is a mouthful of fun.

Wellfleet, MA

TASTING PROFILE

BRINE

SWEETNESS

MINERALITY

NOSE

FINISH

TEXTURE

✓ FIRM

✓ DENSE

✓ MEATY

✓ TOOTHSOME

✓ CRISP

SHELL SIZE

MEAT-TO-SHELL RATIO

PEARL OF WISDOM Blackfish Creek was an epicenter for oysters being shipped from Chesapeake Bay by schooner in the late 1870s. The industry moved to nearby Wellfleet and Boston once the creek became too shallow for the boats to navigate. A few small cottages remain as a reminder of this once prodigious oyster area.

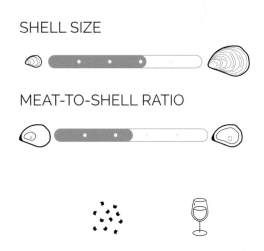

TRY IT WITH A Tobiko topper for a tasty texture. Sip a floral Viognier along with it.

Blue Point

CRASSOSTREA VIRGINICA

MERROIR This quintessential East Coast oyster is the perfect starter oyster for any newbie. The large multi-hued shell says "classic oyster," while the scent plants you on a sunny seaside. It's very consistent with its silky, smooth texture and satisfying liquor. A solid brininess and very fresh, crisp sweetness round out the flavor, leaning into fading eelgrass and salt for the finish. It's the ocean at its finest.

Long Island Sound
New York & Connecticut

TASTING PROFILE

BRINE

SWEETNESS

MINERALITY

NOSE

FINISH

TEXTURE

⊘ LEAN

⊘ SMOOTH

⊘ CRISP

⊘ SILKY

SHELL SIZE

MEAT-TO-SHELL RATIO

PEARL OF WISDOM In the early 1800s, wild Blue Points were famous for their robust flavor and became a favorite of Queen Victoria. The name Blue Point can be used generically today for any oyster along the East Coast, but according to a 1908 law, there can only be one Blue Point Oyster variety.

TRY IT WITH A drop of tabasco and a crisp pilsner or lager to make a classic summer combo.

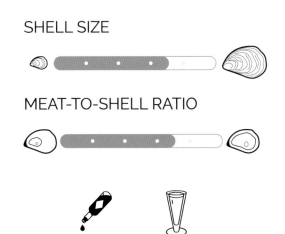

Blue Pool

CRASSOSTREA GIGAS

MERROIR A deep, smooth shell that sits in your hand like a pebble ready to skip across the water. The nose is supremely fragrant, with a scent of florals and melon on wet sand. The bite is big and snappy, hiding a delicate cream amidst a fantastic salted sweet carrot flavor. That delight continues through the finish, making you long for another.

Hammersley Inlet
South Puget Sound, WA

TASTING PROFILE

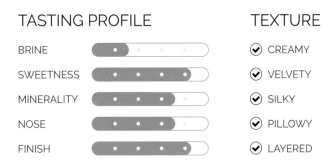

BRINE

SWEETNESS

MINERALITY

NOSE

FINISH

TEXTURE

- ✓ CREAMY
- ✓ VELVETY
- ✓ SILKY
- ✓ PILLOWY
- ✓ LAYERED

PEARL OF WISDOM Shhhh . . . This oyster gets its name from a secret swimming hole of the family who crafts these oysters.

SHELL SIZE

MEAT-TO-SHELL RATIO

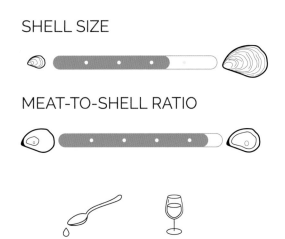

TRY IT WITH A wine mignonette. To drink, mix up a wine slushie with a semi-sweet white. It's pure joy.

Breachway

CRASSOSTREA VIRGINICA

MERROIR Take in the subtle aroma of vegetable broth that glides over the oyster's gorgeous mint-chocolate-chip-colored shell. Breachways tend to be wonderfully consistent in size and shape. The plump meat glistens and brims from edge to edge. Be ready for a fantastic bite, one that bursts with invigorating salt and a tinge of sweetness. Revel in a smooth, crisp, and clean finish that holds on to all that wonderful essence.

Ninigret Pond
Charlestown, RI

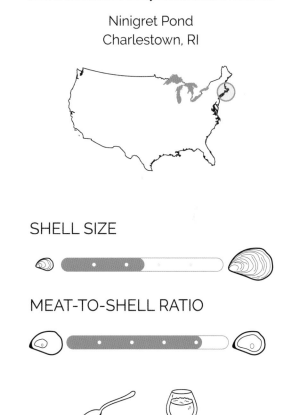

TASTING PROFILE

BRINE	
SWEETNESS	
MINERALITY	
NOSE	
FINISH	

TEXTURE

- ✓ MEATY
- ✓ SPRINGY
- ✓ SATINY
- ✓ CRISP

SHELL SIZE

MEAT-TO-SHELL RATIO

PEARL OF WISDOM Brian Pinsky, owner of the 401 Oyster Co, which harvests Breachways, chose the name "after a lot of brainstorming. I wanted a name that was ocean/marine related and also gave some sort of geographical location in it. Around southern Rhode Island people are very familiar with 'the breachway,' which is in reference to the Charlestown breachway, the opening that brings water in and out of Ninigret Pond."

TRY IT WITH A pickled-pear mignonette for a salty sweet balance. Pair with a robust farmhouse ale.

Cape May Salt

CRASSOSTREA VIRGINICA

MERROIR Cape Mays look like the quintessential oyster, with a shell rolling with off-white and mint-green tones. Beautiful contrasting meat with lots of briny liquor fills the shell. The body is fantastically light and crisp with a deliciously plump and firm bite. Hints of sweet butteriness linger softly, accompanied by an underlying salt flavor and a hint of a metallic taste before easing into a soft finish.

Cape May, NJ

TASTING PROFILE

BRINE

SWEETNESS

MINERALITY

NOSE

FINISH

TEXTURE

✓ CRISP

✓ CLEAN

✓ MEATY

✓ LAYERED

✓ SILKY

SHELL SIZE

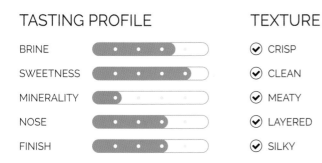

MEAT-TO-SHELL RATIO

PEARL OF WISDOM Cape May oyster production, at its peak, supplied Philadelphia with over 2 million bushels a year. There was such a surplus of oysters that the streets in early colonial Philly were paved with leftover shells. After battling disease, pollution, and overharvesting in the twentieth century, New Jersey oysters are once again seeing a boom.

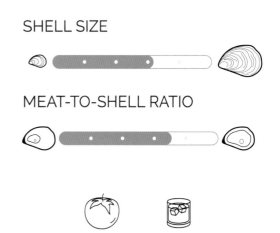

TRY IT WITH A diced Jersey tomato. Pair it with a classic Salty Dog cocktail.

Capital

CRASSOSTREA GIGAS

MERROIR Immediately noticeable is this oyster's impeccable shell uniformity. The shells have a gorgeous texture and color with deep cups from tide tumbling. A sublime fragrance of melon and ocean hits the nose, while the gorgeous meat is drenched in a supremely fresh liquor. Let it swirl before biting into the smooth textured meat, rich with vegetable broth undertones. Crisp, sea-salt flavors accompany wonderful melon rind tones that roll around in your mouth for a long-lingering and delicious finish.

Spencer Cove
Olympia, WA

TASTING PROFILE

BRINE

SWEETNESS

MINERALITY

NOSE

FINISH

TEXTURE

⊘ VELVETY

⊘ TENDER

⊘ TOOTHSOME

⊘ CRISP

SHELL SIZE

MEAT-TO-SHELL RATIO

PEARL OF WISDOM Capital Oyster's master farmer, Tom Bloomfield, is a fifth-generation oysterman. He has spent his life's work building on the knowledge his ancestors passed down to him.

TRY IT WITH A pineapple-mint granita topping, paired with a pineapple-infused vodka.

Chatham

CRASSOSTREA VIRGINICA

MERROIR Chatham shells tend to be consistent, with a teardrop shape and faded color. The subtle, sweet aroma of misty morning wafts over the oyster, swaddled in the shell and bathed in a liquor that provides a nice briny punch. The meat is plump with a delightful bite that elegantly transitions to a delicate sweetness. Make sure to chew this one properly. A perfect balance of salt and sweetness, with a lingering brine flavor, awaits the taste buds.

Oyster River, Chatham
Cape Cod, MA

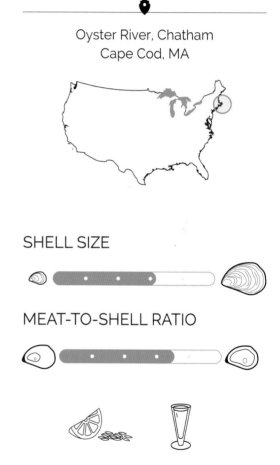

TASTING PROFILE

BRINE

SWEETNESS

MINERALITY

NOSE

FINISH

TEXTURE

- ✓ SNAPPY
- ✓ BURSTING
- ✓ CLEAN
- ✓ FULL-BODIED
- ✓ SMOOTH

SHELL SIZE

MEAT-TO-SHELL RATIO

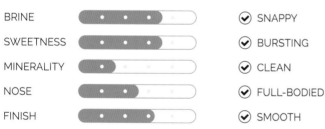

PEARL OF WISDOM Begun in 1976, Chatham Shellfish Company has been a revitalizing force of aquaculture in the region. Revisiting techniques of old, when oyster grants lined the Oyster River and Oyster Pond, incorporating genuinely self-made technology, they've forged a successful modern-day shellfish farming venture.

TRY IT WITH A dabble of orange pulp on top, and wash down with a crisp pilsner.

Chelsea Gem

CRASSOSTREA GIGAS

MERROIR The buttery, toffee ripples of the deep-cupped smooth shell are mesmerizing. The peach flesh stowing away inside is aromatic, with saccharine and subtle salts. A tender bite uncovers a touch of minerality and light cream to start things off, while a sugary and savory liquor dances throughout. The plump and velvety mouthfeel is sublime, with a very smooth saltwater-taffy flavor to cap it all.

Eld Inlet
South Puget Sound, WA

TASTING PROFILE

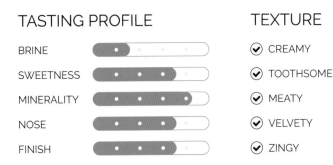

BRINE

SWEETNESS

MINERALITY

NOSE

FINISH

TEXTURE

- ✓ CREAMY
- ✓ TOOTHSOME
- ✓ MEATY
- ✓ VELVETY
- ✓ ZINGY

SHELL SIZE

MEAT-TO-SHELL RATIO

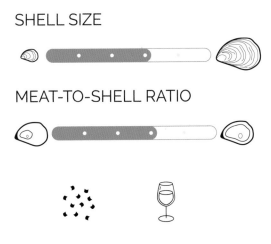

PEARL OF WISDOM Owners and siblings Shina Wysocki & Kyle Lentz are second-generation oyster farmers, part of the growing Washington Shellfish Initiative. A collaboration between state and federal government, tribes, and other shellfish growers, the Initiative protects coastal habitats and water quality.

TRY IT WITH A dash of fresh grated horseradish. Pair with a Chenin Blanc.

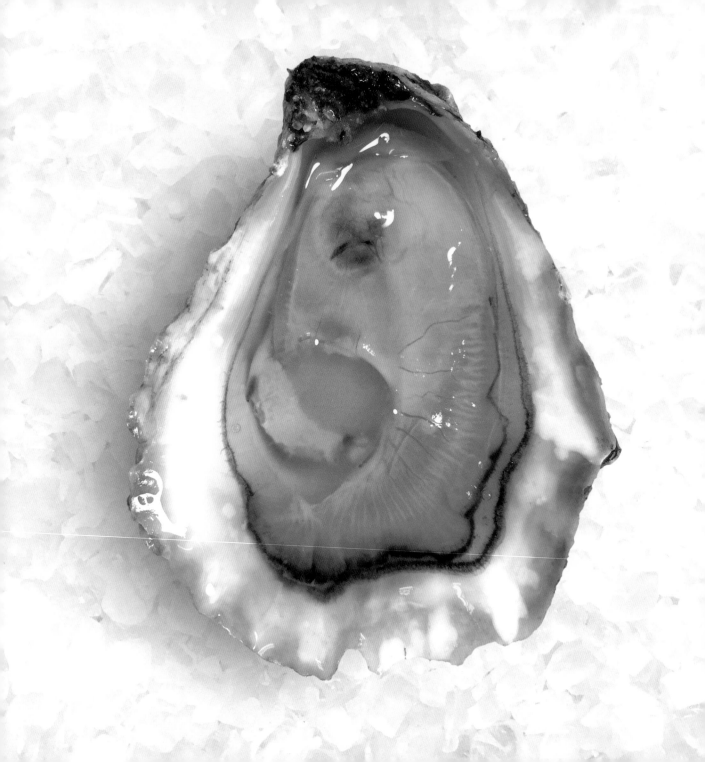

Chincoteague

CRASSOSTREA VIRGINICA

MERROIR A substantial sprawling shell has a nice tear-drop shape and houses a dense, blond-toned meat inside. Its whisper of silt and wet earth is on the nose. The liquor is more subtle than most oysters, but has the distinctive brine of the region it grew up in. Its great bite has gentler tones of sweetness and brine throughout, while the wrap-up is quick with hints of metal.

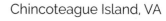

Chincoteague Island, VA

TASTING PROFILE

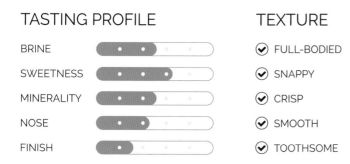

BRINE

SWEETNESS

MINERALITY

NOSE

FINISH

TEXTURE

- ✓ FULL-BODIED
- ✓ SNAPPY
- ✓ CRISP
- ✓ SMOOTH
- ✓ TOOTHSOME

SHELL SIZE

MEAT-TO-SHELL RATIO

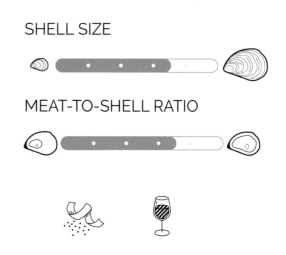

PEARL OF WISDOM In the early days of oyster farming, Chincoteague was a popular choice as a place to culture oysters, to crank up the salinity for Gulf oysters headed north, due to its maze of natural and man-made inlets that fully display the salinity of the Atlantic.

TRY IT WITH A twist of orange peel zest. Pair with a gently sweet rosé.

Choptank Sweet

CRASSOSTREA VIRGINICA

MERROIR Picking up the iridescent shell tinged with gold, a wonderful aroma of a freshwater Chesapeake Bay morning greets the nose. The liquor nearly overflows the shell, washing over a meaty bite with a delightful butter color. A sip reveals subtle brine while the oyster itself has a sweet cream flavor and light texture that balances quite nicely. Moderate salinity and touches of bay grass appear on the finish and fade delicately.

Choptank River
Chesapeake Bay, MD

TASTING PROFILE

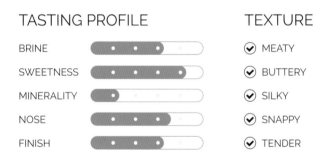

BRINE

SWEETNESS

MINERALITY

NOSE

FINISH

TEXTURE

- ✓ MEATY
- ✓ BUTTERY
- ✓ SILKY
- ✓ SNAPPY
- ✓ TENDER

SHELL SIZE

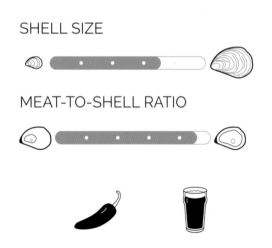

MEAT-TO-SHELL RATIO

PEARL OF WISDOM Choptank Oyster Company produces an average of 1 to 2 million oysters per year and has several million oysters sitting in the bay at any one time, each one acting as a natural filter to remove large volumes of excess nutrients that have plagued the bay from past overharvesting of wild oysters.

TRY IT WITH A finely diced jalapeño. Pair with an oyster stout to make your taste buds dance.

Church Point

CRASSOSTREA GIGAS

MERROIR A wavy shell, filled with deep hues of green and bronze. The meat is a gorgeous bright ivory with contrasting cilia and fills the shell wonderfully. Catch the fragrant scents of seagrass and wildflower before sipping the subtle liquor. Distinct cucumber and melon flavors quickly hit the palate with a silky texture that floats over the tongue. Give it a moment to linger and then segue into a modest sweetness on the finish.

Hammersley Inlet, WA

TASTING PROFILE

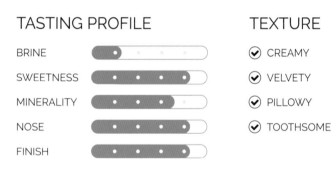

BRINE

SWEETNESS

MINERALITY

NOSE

FINISH

TEXTURE

✓ CREAMY

✓ VELVETY

✓ PILLOWY

✓ TOOTHSOME

SHELL SIZE

MEAT-TO-SHELL RATIO

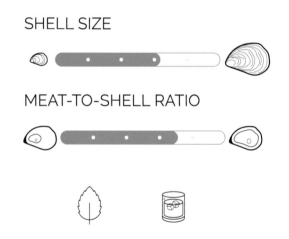

PEARL OF WISDOM As the weather gets cooler, oysters will chow down and fatten up in preparation for winter hibernation. All that food converts into glycogen, a sugar that helps to make oysters tastier.

TRY IT WITH A sliver of mint. Pair with a traditional mojito.

Copps Island

CRASSOSTREA VIRGINICA

MERROIR Get a good whiff of the light, airy sweetness of this lovely oyster. Wonderfully chubby meat fills the shell from edge to edge, with plenty of liquor to savor. A swift burst of brine hits the palate. The bite of the meat is sublime, as the natural sugars run over your taste buds, followed by a faint hint of tin. The flavor finishes fast with a last hit of brine that vanishes just as quickly as it appears. A blissful experience.

Norwalk Islands, CT

TASTING PROFILE

BRINE	●●●
SWEETNESS	●●
MINERALITY	
NOSE	●●
FINISH	●

TEXTURE

- ✓ SILKY
- ✓ SLIPPERY
- ✓ BUTTERY
- ✓ TENDER

SHELL SIZE

MEAT-TO-SHELL RATIO

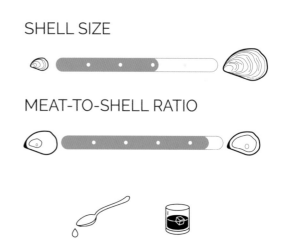

PEARL OF WISDOM Bottom planting, rather than cage or floating trays, gives Copps Island oysters a greater variety of flavors, whereas hatchery oysters tend to be extremely consistent. The focus is on crafting voluminous, plump, shell-filling meats.

TRY IT WITH A roasted shallot mignonette. To drink, try a Negroni.

Cotuit

CRASSOSTREA VIRGINICA

MERROIR The nose hints at fresh grass and a summer vegetable garden. The beautiful teardrop shell is home to delectable clean meat nestled in ample amounts of liquor. The first taste showcases a delicate metallic flavor with tasty brine. Tender meat greets the palate with a soft, yet silky, bite. A light copper finish hangs around briefly before gently dissipating.

Cotuit Bay, MA

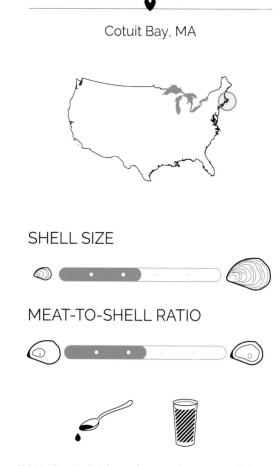

TASTING PROFILE

BRINE	●●●
SWEETNESS	●●
MINERALITY	●●
NOSE	●●
FINISH	●●

TEXTURE

- ✓ MEATY
- ✓ TENDER
- ✓ SILKY
- ✓ SNAPPY
- ✓ LAYERED

SHELL SIZE

MEAT-TO-SHELL RATIO

PEARL OF WISDOM The Cotuit Oyster Company can lay claim to being one of the oldest oyster farms in the United States, with its origins dating back to 1857.

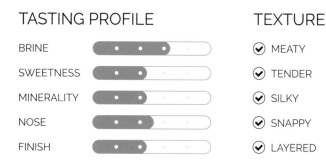

TRY IT WITH A raspberry mignonette. Pair with a Lambic beer.

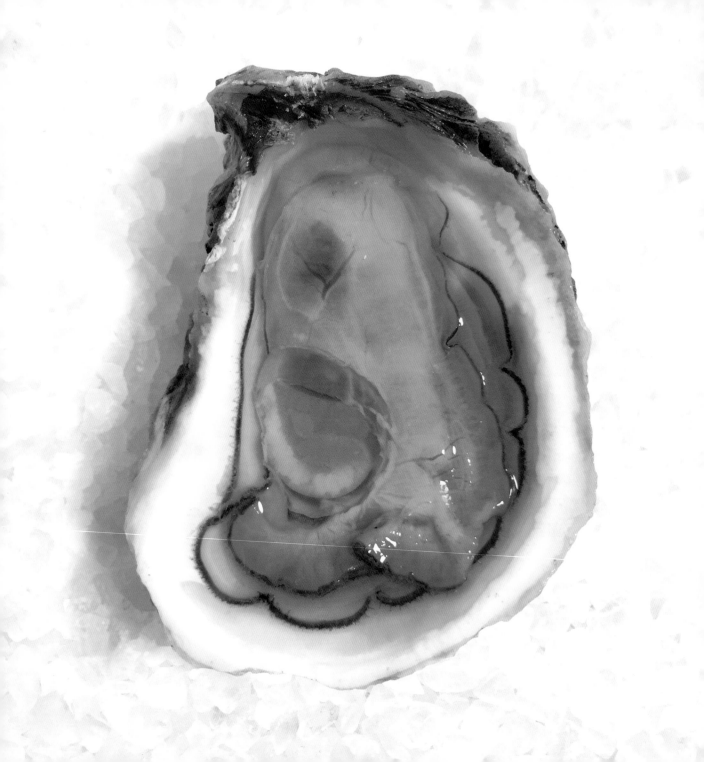

Cup Cake

CRASSOSTREA VIRGINICA

MERROIR Picking up this oyster is almost a workout. The large, rocky shell is dense, but behold the bounty within! The meat is plentiful and fills the shell wonderfully with lots of liquor. A delicate scent of low tide greets the nose and a taste of the liquor reveals a solid brine. The bite is firm throughout with medium brine and soft minerality rolling over the palate. Light, lingering finish.

Oyster Bay, NY

TASTING PROFILE

BRINE	▓▓▓░░
SWEETNESS	▓▓▓▓░
MINERALITY	▓░░░░
NOSE	▓▓░░░
FINISH	▓▓░░░

TEXTURE

- ✓ FULL-BODIED
- ✓ TENDER
- ✓ SLIPPERY
- ✓ SILKY
- ✓ CLEAN

SHELL SIZE

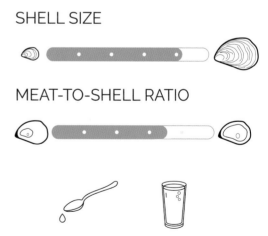

MEAT-TO-SHELL RATIO

PEARL OF WISDOM New York Harbor was the epicenter of oysters in the early nineteenth century and may have contained nearly half the world's oysters at one point. The supply was so robust and the oysters so in-demand, harvests were shipped to the Midwest by train and across the pond to England via steamship.

TRY IT WITH A pear mignonette. A crisp pear cider to wash it down is illuminating.

Daisy Bay

CRASSOSTREA VIRGINICA

MERROIR A wispy wildflower fragrance emanates from a rich burgundy shaded shell. Enclosed within is a glistening and luscious liquor layered with light yet vibrant salinity that weaves through the taste buds. The meat of this oyster is dynamic and hearty, blending a touch of creamy butter over tinges of simple sweetness leaving the palate with a fading finish shifting between muted sugars and delicate ocean vegetals.

Rustico, Hunter River
Prince Edward Island, Canada

TASTING PROFILE

BRINE	
SWEETNESS	
MINERALITY	
NOSE	
FINISH	

TEXTURE

✓ CRISP
✓ TENDER
✓ SILKY
✓ BURSTING
✓ CLEAN

SHELL SIZE

MEAT-TO-SHELL RATIO

PEARL OF WISDOM An oyster's flavor can vary from day to day, even hour to hour, based on the water that it's in. Currents and weather affect the algae and food particles that an oyster feeds on, giving the oyster its unique taste.

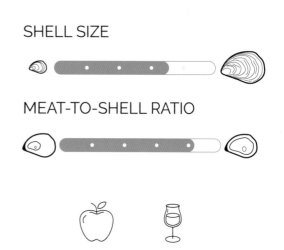

TRY IT WITH A sprinkle of diced apple or a daub of applesauce. Sip ice wine, like a dessert Riesling, to work salty-sweet wonders.

Dune Shadow

CRASSOSTREA VIRGINICA

MERROIR Befitting their name, the shells are a lovely teardrop shape, with rich colors of chocolate brown and grass green. A soft aroma hints at lettuce. The liquor is abundant to the point of overflowing, and surrounds silky meat. The initial flavor is of a very mild brine with a subtle bite, and a burst of saltwater taffy sweetness. The finish is smooth and gratifyingly salty.

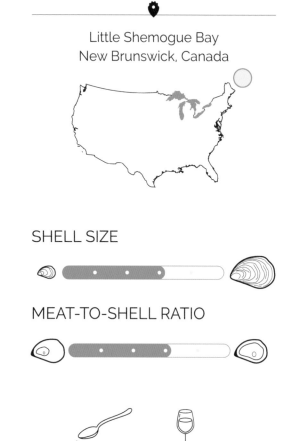

Little Shemogue Bay
New Brunswick, Canada

TASTING PROFILE

BRINE

SWEETNESS

MINERALITY

NOSE

FINISH

TEXTURE

- ✓ SILKY
- ✓ LEAN
- ✓ BURSTING
- ✓ SPRINGY

SHELL SIZE

MEAT-TO-SHELL RATIO

PEARL OF WISDOM The Acadian Peninsula where Dune Shadows grow is pretty much the most northerly point Virginica oysters can call home. Since the water here is cold throughout most of the year, it can take up to five years or more for these oysters to reach market size. The benefit for farmers? They're easier to craft with consistency, because they grow slowly.

TRY IT WITH A honey-cayenne mignonette. Pour a light, mineral Riesling for a refreshing accompaniment.

Eagle Rock

CRASSOSTREA GIGAS

MERROIR Starting with an aromatic scent of melon and damp sod after an evening rainstorm, the plump and paunchy cream-colored meat with darkly contrasting cilia snuggles cozily into a deep, rounded shell. The liquor fills from edge to edge, brimming with brine and metallics. A good chomp reveals wonderful notes of sweetness and vegetals, while a delightful richness rolls over the tongue. Lingering hints of dampened seaweed and subtle melon finish off this fantastic oyster.

Totten Inlet
Puget Sound, WA

TASTING PROFILE

BRINE	
SWEETNESS	
MINERALITY	
NOSE	
FINISH	

TEXTURE

- ✓ LAYERED
- ✓ CREAMY
- ✓ FULL-BODIED
- ✓ TENDER
- ✓ VELVETY

SHELL SIZE

MEAT-TO-SHELL RATIO

PEARL OF WISDOM These oysters take their name from the imposing presence known as Eagle Rock, a locally known perch for the impressive predators who make their home in the area.

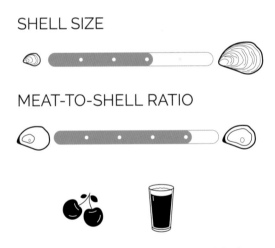

TRY IT WITH A pinch some diced black cherries on top. Drink it up with a smoky stout.

Effingham Inlet

CRASSOSTREA GIGAS

MERROIR Nicknamed the "Effing Oyster," these are not only substantial in size, but also in flavor. The shell has a sensational array of colors and curves, housing pristine and portly meat, glistening with liquor. A delightful aroma of cucumber can be detected. A big bite with a fantastic crunch reveals a burst of Bibb lettuce and touches of brine within the silky, smooth texture. Definitely a mouthful, this oyster sparkles with tones of melon rind and salt on the finish. Effing good!

Vancouver Island
British Columbia, Canada

TASTING PROFILE

BRINE	▓▓░░░
SWEETNESS	▓▓▓▓░
MINERALITY	▓▓▓░░
NOSE	▓▓▓▓░
FINISH	▓▓▓▓░

TEXTURE

- ✓ CREAMY
- ✓ SILKY
- ✓ VELVETY
- ✓ CRUNCHY
- ✓ BURSTING

SHELL SIZE

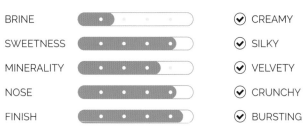

MEAT-TO-SHELL RATIO

PEARL OF WISDOM Owner Mica Verbrugge is very proud of his farm in Barkley Sound. "It sits in a deep-water fjord surrounded by old-growth rain forest . . . 60 km from the nearest paved road and there are no farms, septic fields, cities, major rivers, anywhere near the farm. It combines the biggest rainfalls in North America with deep water upwelling. It's the most pristine location imaginable."

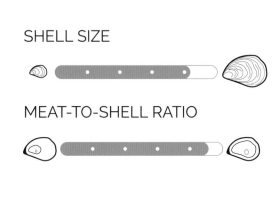

TRY IT WITH Finely diced cucumber with a hit of Thai basil. Pairing with absinthe (either straight or in a cocktail) makes for a radiant flavor combination.

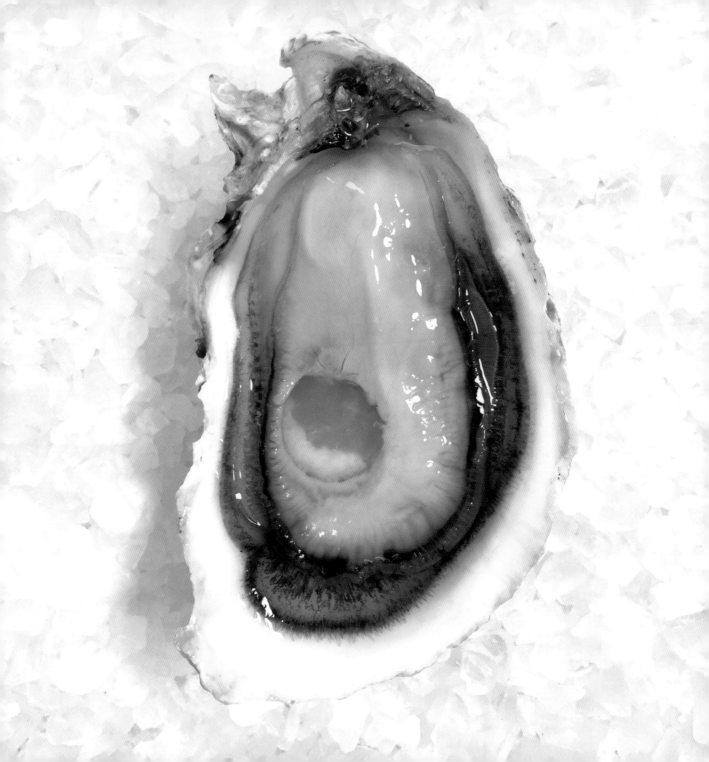

Fanny Bay

CRASSOSTREA GIGAS

MERROIR The large, pearlescent fluted shell could be mistaken for an ancient musical instrument. Opening one is like unlocking a treasure chest. Vibrant notes of seaspray swirl around the picture-perfect meat lounging inside. Slurping this oyster brings to mind snacking on a fresh cucumber with a sprinkle of salt. The portly, plump body has a creamy texture. The finish is bright and crisp with fresh garden notes.

Fanny Bay & Baynes Sound
East Vancouver Island, BC

TASTING PROFILE

BRINE	●●○○○
SWEETNESS	●●●○○
MINERALITY	●●●●○
NOSE	●●●●○
FINISH	●●●●○

TEXTURE

- ✓ MEATY
- ✓ CREAMY
- ✓ VELVETY
- ✓ FULL-BODIED
- ✓ ZINGY

SHELL SIZE

MEAT-TO-SHELL RATIO

PEARL OF WISDOM Considered a quintessential oyster from British Columbia, Canada, the Fanny Bay was one of the first from this region to have widespread availability to eaters and remains extremely popular.

TRY IT WITH Grapefruit pulp (those juicy little containers inside the slices) sprinkled on top. A pour of Ungava gin from Canada with a wedge of cucumber to nibble on makes for a seismic pairing.

Fat Dog

CRASSOSTREA VIRGINICA

MERROIR It starts with a wonderful nose of a fresh spring breeze on the bay. The meat sits in deep-cupped and pristine shells, speckled with copper tones. The liquor provides an intense briny kick that quickly reveals its sweetness. A delicious, tender bite with wonderful hints of grass and greens sprinkled with salt rolls sublimely around the palate. The lingering finish is bright and crisp. This is a fantastic New Hampshire oyster.

Great Bay, NH

TASTING PROFILE

BRINE

SWEETNESS

MINERALITY

NOSE

FINISH

TEXTURE

- ✓ LEAN
- ✓ CRISP
- ✓ TENDER
- ✓ SLIPPERY

SHELL SIZE

MEAT-TO-SHELL RATIO

PEARL OF WISDOM Sometimes a best friend inspires a name. In this case, man's best friend. The farm is affectionately named after the founders' retriever.

TRY IT WITH Diced-up grilled peach and red onion for a revelatory accompaniment. Grab a frosty English Olde Ale–style brew and kick back.

Fiddler's Cove

CRASSOSTREA VIRGINICA

MERROIR Tucked neatly into the vivid tiger-toned shell is an invigorating blast of briny liquor that washes over the palate. Tender meat reveals a subtle, sweet syrup and slight nickel flavor, while the finish is refreshing and near-pristine with just a touch of metallic flavor staying behind. A drop of lemon complements this oyster perfectly.

Megansett Harbor
North Falmouth, MA

TASTING PROFILE

BRINE	●●●
SWEETNESS	●●●
MINERALITY	●●
NOSE	●●
FINISH	●●●

TEXTURE

- ✓ ZINGY
- ✓ SILKY
- ✓ LEAN
- ✓ BURSTING
- ✓ SPRINGY

SHELL SIZE

MEAT-TO-SHELL RATIO

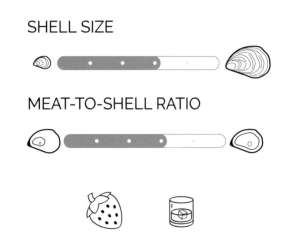

PEARL OF WISDOM Ward Aquafarms not only has produced oysters like Fiddler's Cove since 2012, but it also puts significant effort into researching new species to culture, designing new culture methods, and expanding aquaculture production in New England.

TRY IT WITH A sliver of fresh strawberry. Sip a sumptuous smoky mezcal.

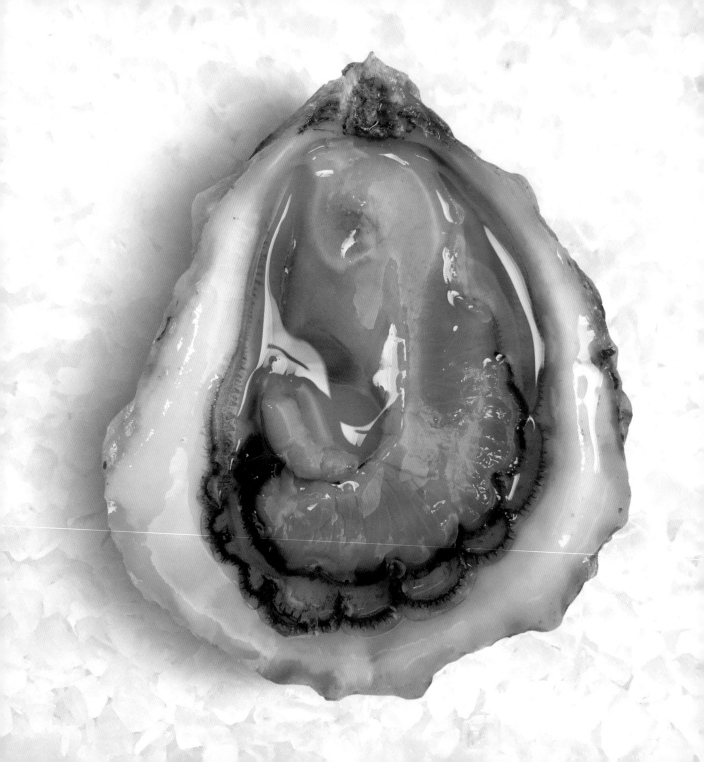

Fishers Island

CRASSOSTREA VIRGINICA

MERROIR The first sip of liquor is pure, robust salt, while the bite is crisp and refreshingly clean. Let this one roll around the palate while the lean texture gives way to a delicately sweet flavor. The finish is wonderful with a light sweetness that fades gently and urges you to reach for another. Take note of the consistently beautiful round shells with hints of bronze and eggshell along with the gorgeous scalloping.

Fishers Island, NY

TASTING PROFILE

BRINE

SWEETNESS

MINERALITY

NOSE

FINISH

TEXTURE

⊘ BUTTERY

⊘ MEATY

⊘ SMOOTH

⊘ VELVETY

⊘ CLEAN

SHELL SIZE

MEAT-TO-SHELL RATIO

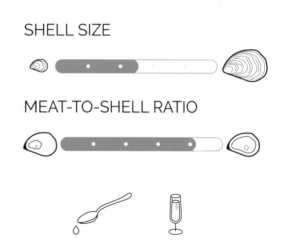

PEARL OF WISDOM Fishers Island Oyster Farm has been growing shellfish for 35 years. They also produce oyster seed for over 50 other farmers!

TRY IT WITH A Prosecco mignonette along with, what else, Prosecco to sip on. Simple is powerful here.

Flapjack Point

CRASSOSTREA GIGAS

MERROIR This deep-cupped, fluted shell is ribboned with candy stripes of green, purple, bronze, and black. The shell is beautiful enough by itself, but it also holds a gorgeous vanilla, almost black-edged oyster with a wonderfully fragrant melon bouquet. Soaking in a zesty zinc liquor, the meat has a fantastic bite, full of melon rind flavoring and a delectable buttery texture. The melon and slate blend lingers through the finish with notes of nori on the end.

Eld Inlet
Puget Sound, WA

TASTING PROFILE

BRINE

SWEETNESS

MINERALITY

NOSE

FINISH

TEXTURE

⊘ CREAMY

⊘ BURSTING

⊘ ZESTY

⊘ ZINGY

SHELL SIZE

MEAT-TO-SHELL RATIO

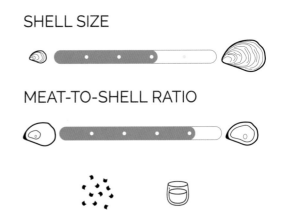

PEARL OF WISDOM Oysters are the most valuable shellfish resource in Washington State. Farming was revitalized in the late 1800s by the introduction of the Pacific oyster from Japan, a variety that spread throughout the region.

TRY IT WITH A pinch of dried nori flakes on top. Sip a dry, crisp sake for a sublime pairing.

Forty North Rose Cove

CRASSOSTREA VIRGINICA

MERROIR These ornamental ivory-colored shells with charcoal lines are little works of art. An aroma of breezy summer seaside is unmistakable. The liquor is overflowing both with volume and salty flavor. A gorgeous, pale golden meat lounges inside, with a lean texture and a pop of brine that bounces back-and-forth with a delightful seagrass sweetness. This tussle rolls through the finish for a memorable nosh.

Rose Cove, NJ

TASTING PROFILE

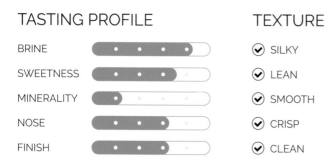

BRINE

SWEETNESS

MINERALITY

NOSE

FINISH

TEXTURE

- ✓ SILKY
- ✓ LEAN
- ✓ SMOOTH
- ✓ CRISP
- ✓ CLEAN

SHELL SIZE

MEAT-TO-SHELL RATIO

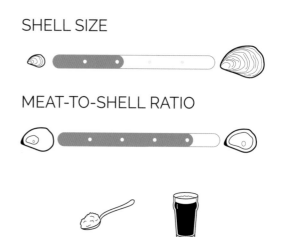

PEARL OF WISDOM "Ninety percent of our business is conducted in ten weeks within a stone's throw of the beach," says Matt Gregg, who owns and runs the oyster farm. "When people come to the [New Jersey] Shore, they want to eat oysters from that place. We hand-pick our oysters with precision. The servers and chefs sell them with passion, because chances are they've been out on the farm with us in hip boots. They know the experience."

TRY IT WITH An iced tropical fruit mignonette with a hint of basil. Pair with an oatmeal milk stout.

Gold Creek

CRASSOSTREA GIGAS

MERROIR A fragrant bouquet of florals and salted honeydew start off on the nose. The meat is notable for its fluttery, dark edges. An initial sip of the overflowing briny liquor uncovers traces of grass and spinach. This oyster has a fantastic chew to it, a silky texture with revelations of creamed spinach and steamed kale on the tongue. An absolutely magnificent flavor holds on tightly to the palate. Be sure to admire the emerald-iridescent scalloped shells. Gold Creeks are true beauties.

Western Inlets
Hood Canal, WA

TASTING PROFILE

BRINE	
SWEETNESS	
MINERALITY	
NOSE	
FINISH	

TEXTURE

- ✓ CREAMY
- ✓ SILKY
- ✓ VELVETY
- ✓ LAYERED
- ✓ ZINGY

SHELL SIZE

MEAT-TO-SHELL RATIO

PEARL OF WISDOM These oysters get their name from the area that was made famous during the golden days. Literally. The boom in this location during the Gold Rush era provided opportunities for wealth and riches, both through gold hunting and oyster raising.

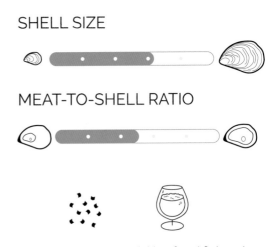

TRY IT WITH A sprinkle of nori flakes. A funky Saison makes a good drink pairing.

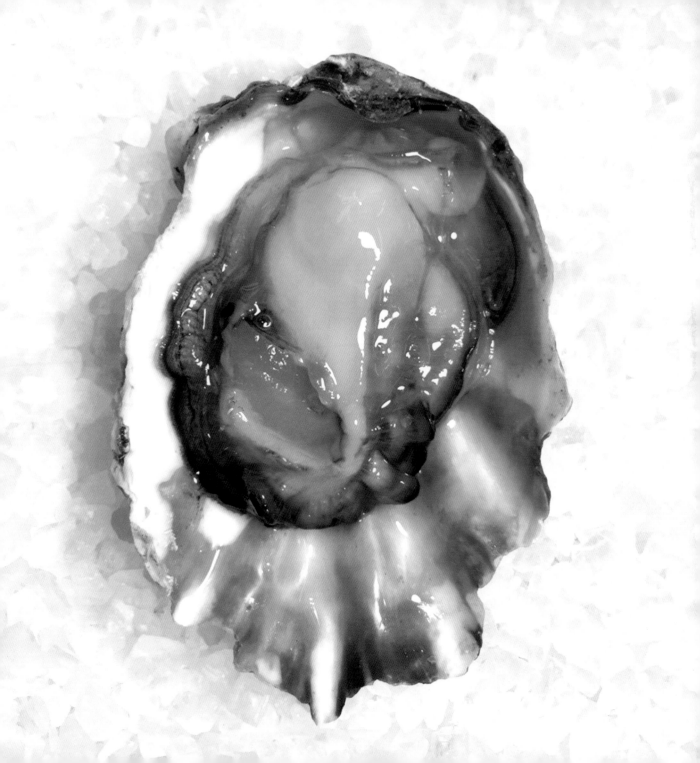

Hama Hama

CRASSOSTREA GIGAS

MERROIR The weather-worn platinum colored shell tells the story behind the crafting of this beach-cultured oyster. First, an eye-opening burst of fresh-cut cucumber dances into the nose. The burly, fleshy meat looks like it belly-flopped into all the liquor inside. You can see gorgeous gradation from edge to center. A memorable bite bursts with citrus tones layered with crisp lettuce amidst a delicate silky cream texture. Ride the wave of airy salty-sweetness until the finish disappears.

Hammersley Inlet
South Puget Sound, WA

TASTING PROFILE

BRINE

SWEETNESS

MINERALITY

NOSE

FINISH

TEXTURE

- ✓ CREAMY
- ✓ PILLOWY
- ✓ TENDER
- ✓ MEATY
- ✓ SMOOTH

SHELL SIZE

MEAT-TO-SHELL RATIO

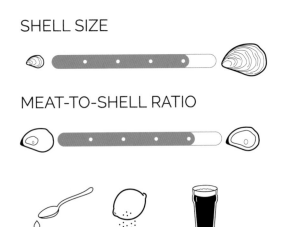

PEARL OF WISDOM Hama Hama sits on property that was purchased for harvesting lumber, not oysters, way back in the 1890s. Now Hama Hama is a fifth-generation family-owned and-operated sustainable shellfish and tree farm. The watershed where it is located is a premium spot for experimenting with techniques and creating a unique merroir.

TRY IT WITH A few drops of gin with lime zest. So tasty! Go with a fruit-tinged session on nitro. The creamy sensation coming from the nitrogen bubbles makes a compelling complement.

Harstine Island

CRASSOSTREA GIGAS

MERROIR The gorgeous shells are lined with a golden pearlescence on the inside. The meat is hefty, colored with tones of bronze and gold, shimmering with the liquor it bathes in. Faint hints of melon and florals dance through the nostrils. The liquor is heavier on the brine than many West Coast oysters, balanced with a wonderful watermelon freshness. Salted melon rind lingers on the finish.

Case Inlet, WA

TASTING PROFILE

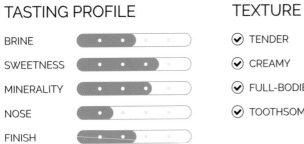

BRINE	
SWEETNESS	
MINERALITY	
NOSE	
FINISH	

TEXTURE

- ✓ TENDER
- ✓ CREAMY
- ✓ FULL-BODIED
- ✓ TOOTHSOME

SHELL SIZE

MEAT-TO-SHELL RATIO

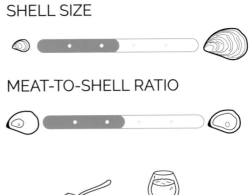

PEARL OF WISDOM The word *ostracized* is derived from ancient Roman times. In order to banish someone from a kingdom, the village elders would vote with oyster shells. A cup up meant you could stay. Cup down? Farewell.

TRY IT WITH A pat of preserved lemon. Try an ale such as a Peche'n'Brett.

Hog Neck Bay

CRASSOSTREA VIRGINICA

MERROIR Hog Necks have tiger-striped shells with beautiful golden hues. The smell of dried seaweed hits the nose. The milky meat is gold-toned with a nice liquor. The bite is soft and meaty. Deep brine flavors lead into a delectable sweetness which recalls buttered steamed kale or Brussels sprouts. The finish is light, with the slightest touch of sugar.

North Fork
Long Island, NY

TASTING PROFILE

BRINE	●●●
SWEETNESS	●●●
MINERALITY	●
NOSE	●●●
FINISH	●

TEXTURE

- ⊘ SNAPPY
- ⊘ SLIPPERY
- ⊘ CRISP
- ⊘ SILKY
- ⊘ TENDER

SHELL SIZE

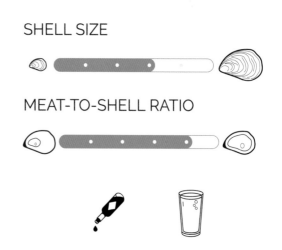

MEAT-TO-SHELL RATIO

PEARL OF WISDOM Oysters love making their homes on craggy coastlines with lots of nooks and crannies. Vital nutrients pool in these areas, meaning the oysters eat well. Because of this, the North and South Forks of Long Island make exceptional areas for oyster cultivation.

TRY IT WITH A dab of hot sauce. Offset the heat with the slightly sour tinge of a Gose.

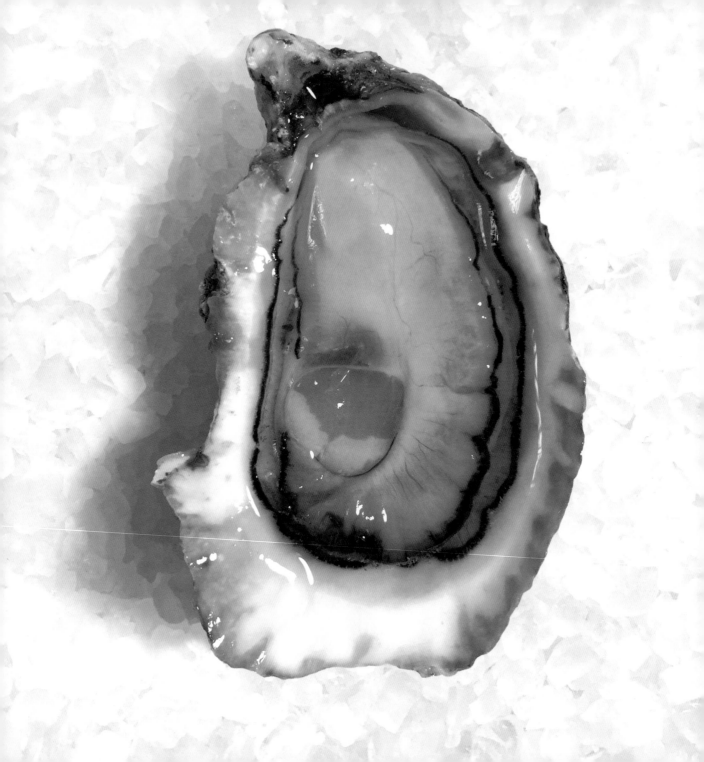

Hollywood

CRASSOSTREA VIRGINICA

MERROIR Like a foggy fall morning on the banks of the Chesapeake, aromatic notes of bay grass and silt greet your nose when you open the black-and-white shell. The deep cup cradles beautiful ivory meat floating in a crisp and mildly sweet liquor. Subtle hints of cucumber sweetness accompany the delectable plump meat. The delightful minerality hangs around on a wonderful finish.

Patuxent River - Chesapeake Bay
Hollywood, MD

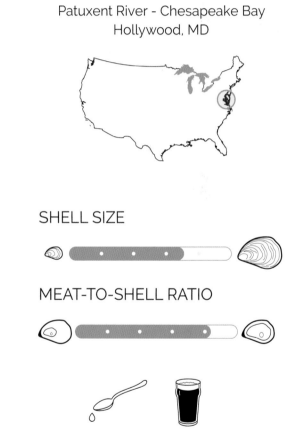

TASTING PROFILE

BRINE

SWEETNESS

MINERALITY

NOSE

FINISH

TEXTURE

✓ BUTTERY

✓ TOOTHSOME

✓ SILKY

✓ MEATY

✓ CRISP

SHELL SIZE

MEAT-TO-SHELL RATIO

PEARL OF WISDOM Before the Hollywood Oyster Company started, the sandy-bottomed creek where the company is located had relatively few fish and crabs. Now rows of oyster cages have created micro-environments with crabs, minnows, mosses, barnacles, and many other biologicals thriving alongside the oysters. Hollywood Oyster Company is pleased to do its part to help restore the Chesapeake Bay.

TRY IT WITH A tangerine-chili mignonette. Drink with a local Chesapeake oyster stout.

Holy Grail

CRASSOSTREA VIRGINICA

MERROIR An undulating toffee-and-fudge cream shell holds a delight. The moist, earthy, garden-soil scent dances over fatty, flaxen-hued meat. Each sip has a robust flavor, and the toothsome bite springs a juicy "just after a spring rain" quality. The silt and savory earthiness lingers in the finish. The merroir is strong in this one.

Hooper Island, MD

TASTING PROFILE

BRINE

SWEETNESS

MINERALITY

NOSE

FINISH

TEXTURE

- ✓ SLIPPERY
- ✓ VELVETY
- ✓ BUTTERY
- ✓ TENDER

SHELL SIZE

MEAT-TO-SHELL RATIO

PEARL OF WISDOM Hooper Island Oyster Aquaculture Company, the producer of the Holy Grail oyster, is developing a sustainable oyster industry in the state of Maryland. This, along with overall efforts of the Maryland seafood industry, will help to re-establish the balance of the Chesapeake Bay.

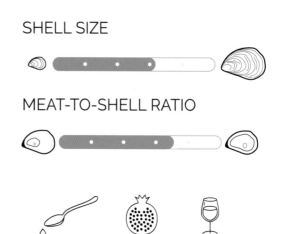

TRY IT WITH A few drops of white wine topped with pomegranate seeds. Imbibe a Muscadet to further enhance the flavors.

Hood Canal

CRASSOSTREA GIGAS

MERROIR These undulating shells are reminiscent of moose horns. The shell is a beautiful rocky gray tinged with green. A robust and fragrant prosciutto and cantaloupe aroma rises from the copious liquor. The pillowy soft, plump meat has a robust bite, with a zing made of zinc, green pepper, and collard greens, and all with a splendid silky texture. Melon, a metallic taste, and a long-lasting creaminess remain through the finish. Take your time with this one.

Western Channels
Hood Canal, WA

TASTING PROFILE

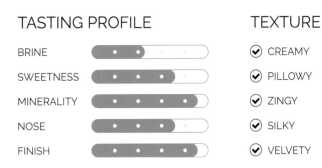

BRINE

SWEETNESS

MINERALITY

NOSE

FINISH

TEXTURE

- ✓ CREAMY
- ✓ PILLOWY
- ✓ ZINGY
- ✓ SILKY
- ✓ VELVETY

SHELL SIZE

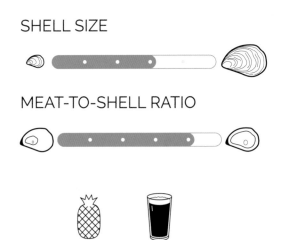

MEAT-TO-SHELL RATIO

PEARL OF WISDOM There are at least 16 varieties of oysters available in the Hood Canal oyster appellation of Washington State. Hood Canal is a natural fjord, and one of four main water regions of Puget Sound. Its waters are pristine and deep, being fed by the majestic Olympic Mountain range.

TRY IT WITH Charred pineapple and diced cucumber. For a heavenly pairing, try drinking it with a chocolate coffee porter.

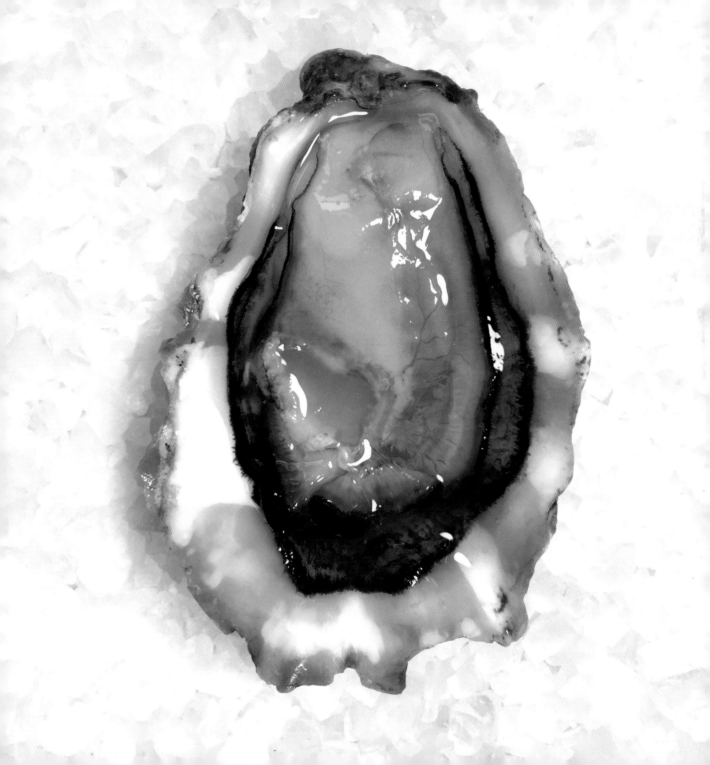

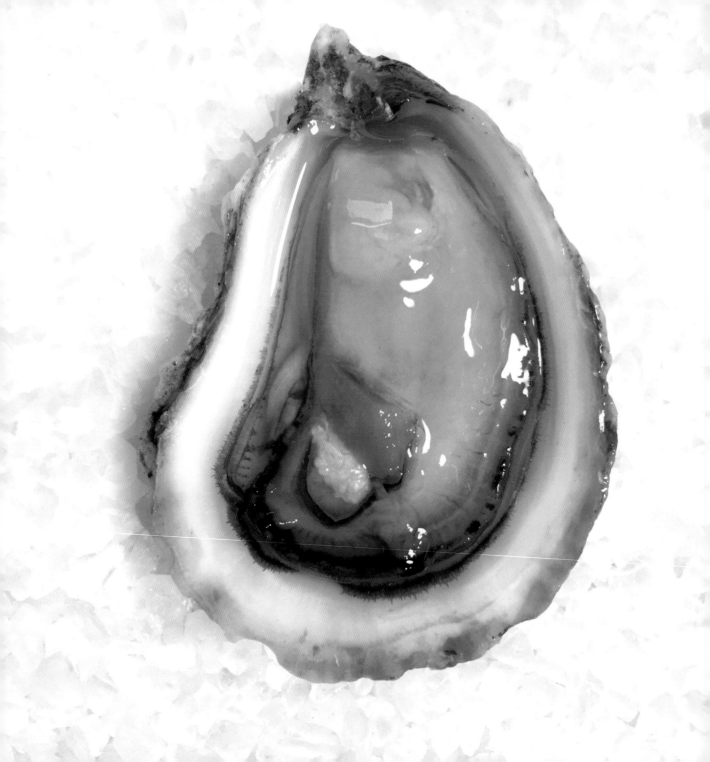

Irish Point

CRASSOSTREA VIRGINICA

MERROIR The petite, alabaster-and-copper–colored teardrop shell is a definite eye-catcher. Take a good whiff of the sweet, breezy aroma of ocean air. The sumptuous meat is surrounded by plenty of sweet briny liquor, rich with hints of iron and copper. The flavor is savory with a fantastic bite, notes of white mushroom, and a superb salty taste as well. The finish is crisp and long-lasting.

Rustico, Hunter River
Prince Edward Island, Canada

TASTING PROFILE

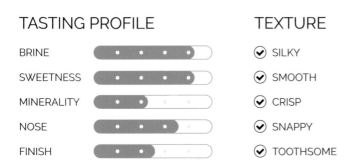

BRINE	
SWEETNESS	
MINERALITY	
NOSE	
FINISH	

TEXTURE

- ⊘ SILKY
- ⊘ SMOOTH
- ⊘ CRISP
- ⊘ SNAPPY
- ⊘ TOOTHSOME

SHELL SIZE

MEAT-TO-SHELL RATIO

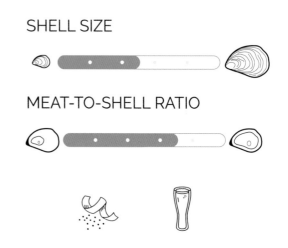

PEARL OF WISDOM Irish Points are part of the Raspberry Point Oyster Co., which also sells oysters under the Daisy Bay, Pickle Point, Lucky Limes, Shiny Sea, and Raspberry Point brands. In total, the company produces nearly 10 million oysters a year.

TRY IT WITH A little twist of lemon. Pair with a lemony Weissbier.

Island Creek

CRASSOSTREA VIRGINICA

MERROIR The exquisite eggshell and toffee-hued shell has rolling muted waves. A vibrant scent of morning moss hits the nostrils, while a sip of the gentle liquor reveals a simple syrupy succulence. The golden meat has a tender, silky bite, bursting when a dollop of salted butter is added. All that wonderful flavor rounds off with a delectably clean, floral essence to relish.

Hunts Flats
Duxbury Bay, MA

TASTING PROFILE

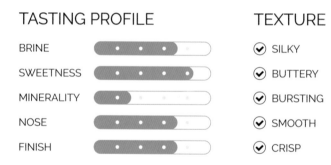

BRINE

SWEETNESS

MINERALITY

NOSE

FINISH

TEXTURE

- ⊘ SILKY
- ⊘ BUTTERY
- ⊘ BURSTING
- ⊘ SMOOTH
- ⊘ CRISP

SHELL SIZE

MEAT-TO-SHELL RATIO

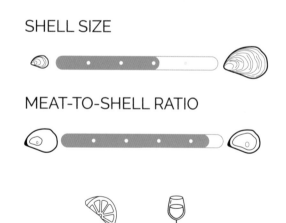

PEARL OF WISDOM Island Creek Oysters are actually not grown in a creek, but in Duxbury Bay. Skip Bennet, the owner, grew up near Island Creek, which flows into Duxbury Bay. Skip was meeting with a chef in the early days of the company when he was asked what the oysters were called. Put on the spot, he said "Island Creek Oysters." The brand has grown from there.

TRY IT WITH The tiniest touch of lemon or other citrus—it works wonders here. Pair with a buttery Chardonnay or a crisp Pinot Gris.

Kumamoto

CRASSOSTREA SIKAMEA

MERROIR Considered the "grand pearl" among oysters, the tiger-paw-shaped shell is its own spectacle to behold. A breathtaking aroma starts, redolent of a foggy day at the beach with wet sand beneath your feet and seaweed washed up on the shoreline. A perennial favorite for its petite meat soaking in a salted melon liquor with a delectable, silky texture. The finishing touch is delightful, delicate, and creamy. Whether you're a beginner or seasoned eater, this oyster is always a treat.

South Puget Sound, WA
or Humboldt Bay, CA

TASTING PROFILE

BRINE

SWEETNESS

MINERALITY

NOSE

FINISH

TEXTURE

- ✓ VELVETY
- ✓ CREAMY
- ✓ PILLOWY
- ✓ BURSTING
- ✓ ZINGY

SHELL SIZE

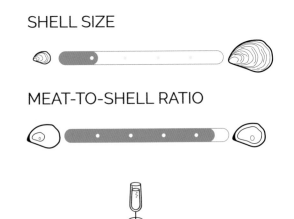

MEAT-TO-SHELL RATIO

PEARL OF WISDOM Kumamotos originated in Japan, but they were never important to the Japanese economy. They only shipped to the US after World War II as a potential replacement for the Olympia. Cross-breeding with Pacific oysters nearly wiped out genetically pure stock until a few wild, pure specimens surfaced in the early 1990s.

TRY IT WITH Nothing. Avoid any extra accoutrements and savor the flavor. As a drink pairing, try Champagne—Kumamotos deserve only the best.

Kusshi

CRASSOSTREA GIGAS

MERROIR These deep-cupped little doozies are a great West Coast oyster for newbies and connoisseurs alike. They have a supremely floral and melon-y aroma. The liquor is wonderfully sweet with a touch of brine. The meat is plump and pillowy, mildly sweet and creamy, and extremely tender, and the finish is light and clean.

Deep Bay
Vancouver Island, BC

TASTING PROFILE

BRINE	●———
SWEETNESS	●——●——●
MINERALITY	●——●——●
NOSE	●——●——●——●
FINISH	●——●——●

TEXTURE

- ✓ SILKY
- ✓ MEATY
- ✓ CREAMY
- ✓ SMOOTH
- ✓ TENDER

SHELL SIZE

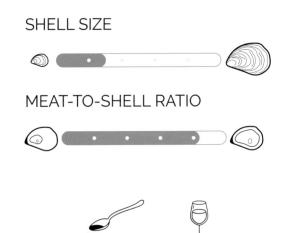

MEAT-TO-SHELL RATIO

PEARL OF WISDOM Kusshi is Japanese for "precious," and the name is totally justified for this oyster. Oyster farmer Keith Reid of Stellar Bay Shellfish Farm crafts this oyster with aggressive tumbling to create a smooth shell with a cup almost as deep as it is long.

TRY IT WITH A touch of Ponzu. Pair with a fruit-forward Riesling for a palate-pleasing pop.

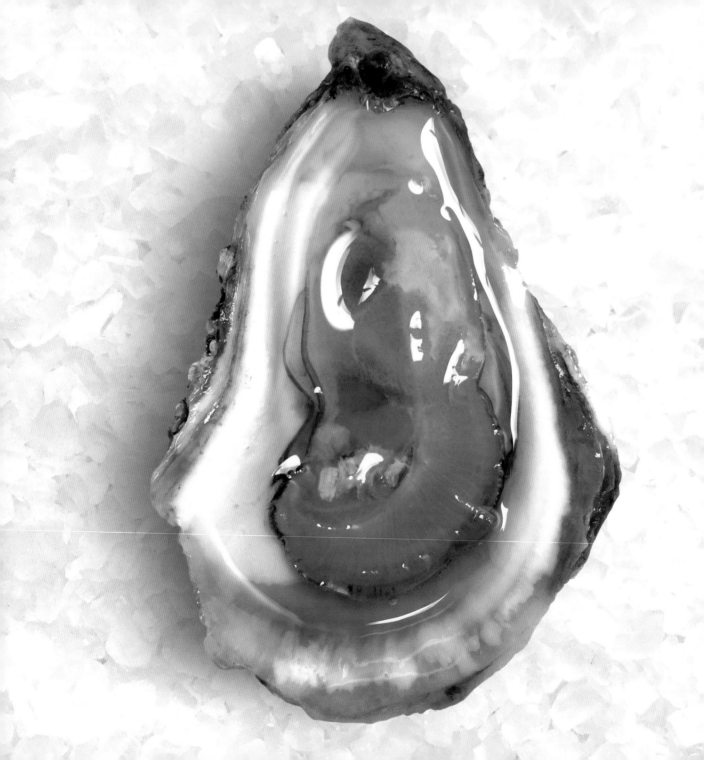

Lady Chatterley

CRASSOSTREA VIRGINICA

MERROIR A delicate bouquet of ocean mist and sea breeze wafts into the nose. Snuggled into the shell is a delicate, ivory meat that soaks in lots of light brine liquor. The bite is very lean and easy, with a nice touch of salt and some hints of simple syrup. The finish is lightly sweet and fades quickly. Admire the deep-cupped shell, rich with sandy tones and weathered texture.

Northumberland Straight
New Brunswick, Canada

TASTING PROFILE

BRINE
SWEETNESS
MINERALITY
NOSE
FINISH

TEXTURE

- ✓ LEAN
- ✓ SMOOTH
- ✓ CRISP
- ✓ CLEAN

SHELL SIZE

MEAT-TO-SHELL RATIO

PEARL OF WISDOM The Lady Chatterley has an exceptionally strong adductor muscle. These hold the shell together when the oyster is fighting currents and tides. This muscle also makes the Lady Chatterley a tough shuck!

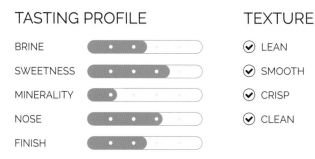

TRY IT WITH A shallot and apple mignonette. Sip on a smooth Canadian whiskey.

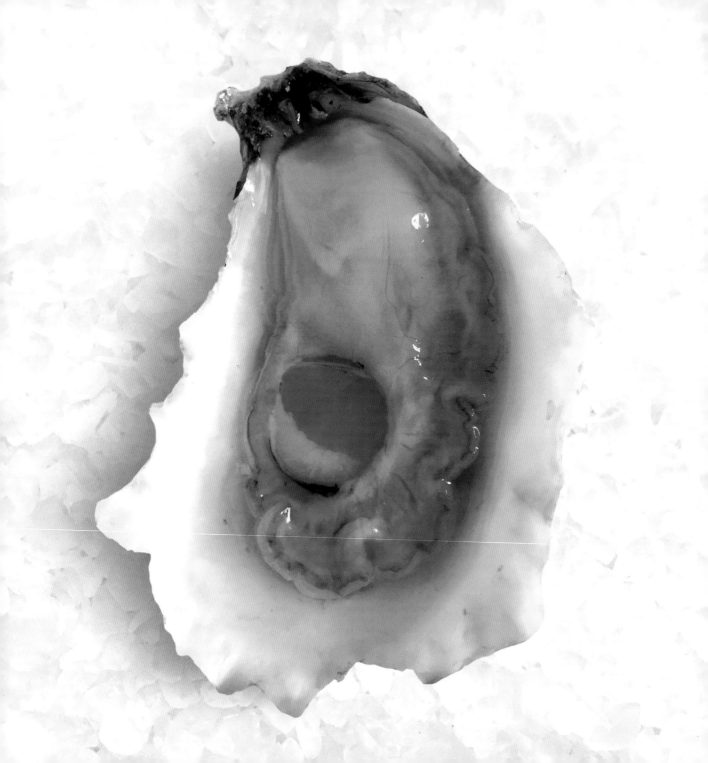

Little Bitches

CRASSOSTREA VIRGINICA

MERROIR This oyster has the aroma of a fresh, wet ocean mist with a subtle hint of florals. Plump meat fills the shell, surrounded by plenty of liquor. Take a sip. The flavor starts off light and mild, while the body is lean with a nice bite. Flavorful hints of damp woodland, with a soft linger of kale and seagrass, accompany the finish. Take note of the flowing shells, which carry a weather-beaten and tidal-grooved look characteristic of the Chesapeake bay where they're farmed.

Magotha Bay, VA

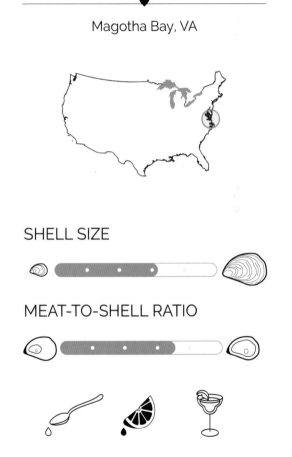

TASTING PROFILE

BRINE	●●○○○
SWEETNESS	●●●○○
MINERALITY	●○○○○
NOSE	●●●○○
FINISH	●●○○○

TEXTURE

- ✓ BUTTERY
- ✓ TOOTHSOME
- ✓ SILKY
- ✓ MEATY
- ✓ CRISP

SHELL SIZE

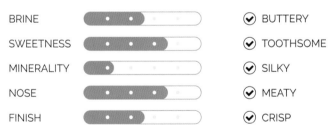

MEAT-TO-SHELL RATIO

PEARL OF WISDOM A sassy oyster deserves a sassy name. A favorite barkeep from Henlopen City Oyster House helped Cobb Station Oysters with this moniker.

TRY IT WITH A little tequila and lime for a zingy topping. For a drink pairing, try a classic margarita.

Little Island

CRASSOSTREA VIRGINICA

MERROIR An out-of-sight pearly-white shell holds a fragrance of moss and pepper. A silky-smooth meat is soaked in a lush liquor with hints of soil and silt. The flavor can be described as a combination of beautifully blended earth and watermelon-rind. This oyster finishes with a delicate moss and vegetal flavor that lingers like a shooting star.

Bagaduce, ME

TASTING PROFILE

BRINE	●●●○
SWEETNESS	●●●○
MINERALITY	●○○○
NOSE	●●●○
FINISH	●○○○

TEXTURE

- ✓ SILKY
- ✓ LEAN
- ✓ SMOOTH
- ✓ CRISP
- ✓ BURSTING

SHELL SIZE

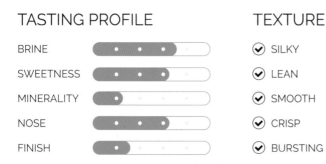

MEAT-TO-SHELL RATIO

PEARL OF WISDOM Who wouldn't want oysters out their front door? The Peasley Family runs this oyster farm right next to their family camp.

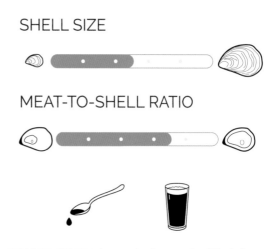

TRY IT WITH A carrot mignonette. Wash it down with an easy drinking Schwarzbier.

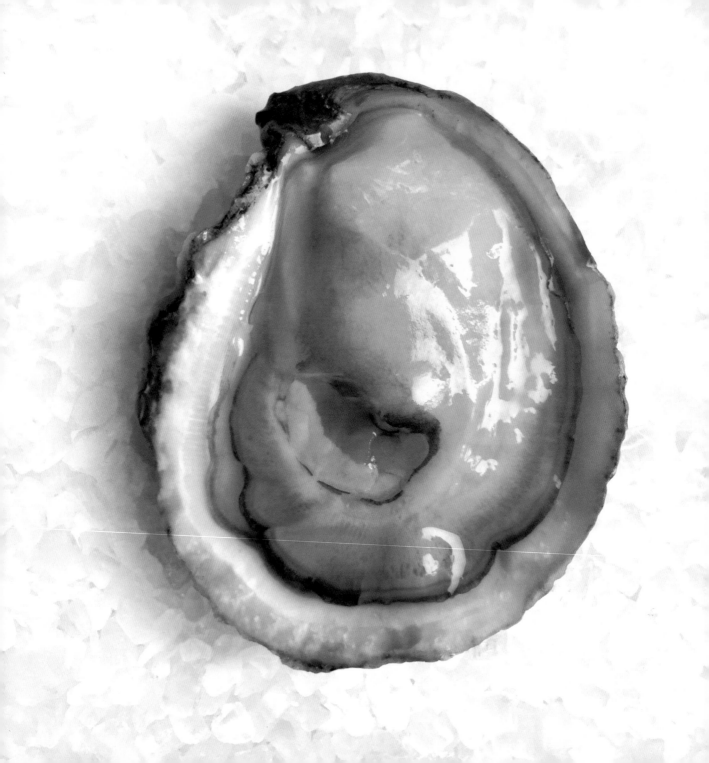

Louisiana

CRASSOSTREA VIRGINICA

MERROIR The heft of the shell is immediately evident. Inside is a gem of an oyster. The light, sweet aroma wafts over a sparkling liquor, reminiscent of a sunlit Gulf Coast morning on the water. The roly-poly meat floats inside the shell. The first sip of liquor reveals a gentle balance of brine and sweetness, while the bite is big and full-bodied. Bouncing layers of creamed spinach flavor capture the merroir of the Gulf. The savory flavor remains for a nice stay before gently fading with hints of simple syrup under the salts.

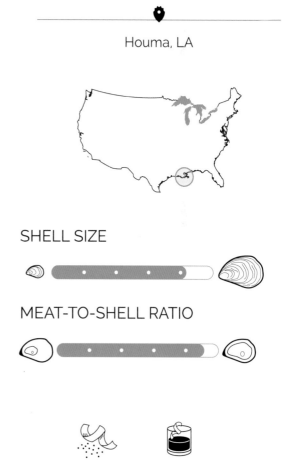

Houma, LA

TASTING PROFILE

BRINE

SWEETNESS

MINERALITY

NOSE

FINISH

TEXTURE

✓ SILKY

✓ BUTTERY

✓ MEATY

✓ CLEAN

✓ CRISP

SHELL SIZE

MEAT-TO-SHELL RATIO

PEARL OF WISDOM Taste and versatility make Louisiana's oysters a culinary classic. Their unique flavor is fed by the nutrient-rich waters of estuaries, served by the Mississippi and Atchafalaya rivers. Connoisseurs savor them raw and served on ice, but they're also enjoyed chargrilled, fried, Bienvilled, Rockerfellered, or as lagniappe to a stew or gumbo.

TRY IT WITH A twist of citrus. Drink a New Orleans classic, the Sazerac.

Malpeque

CRASSOSTREA VIRGINICA

MERROIR The teardrop-shaped shell has a deep bend. The first scent is light and breezy. Inside is a beautiful meat that is brimming edge-to-edge with liquor that has a gentle brine flavor. The body is lean, with a nice, mild flavor revealing a silky texture and subtle tones of nuttiness. The clean, crisp finish has hints of a sweet saltiness. The Malpeque is a classic oyster for beginners and well-seasoned oyster eaters alike.

Malpeque Bay
Prince Edward Island, Canada

TASTING PROFILE

BRINE	●●●
SWEETNESS	●●●
MINERALITY	●
NOSE	●●
FINISH	●●

TEXTURE

- ✓ TENDER
- ✓ SLIPPERY
- ✓ SILKY
- ✓ BURSTING
- ✓ SMOOTH

SHELL SIZE

MEAT-TO-SHELL RATIO

PEARL OF WISDOM There are different variations of the Malpeque oyster from this region of PEI, but the original is considered by many oyster aficionados to be the best of the bunch. Why is this so? The cold, nutrient-laden salinity of the waters all come together to give these oysters their wonderful flavor.

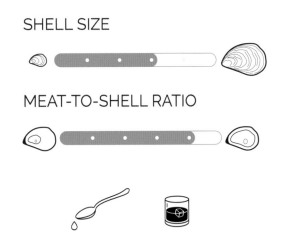

TRY IT WITH A pear and pickled ginger mignonette. Sip a molasses-rich Caribbean rum.

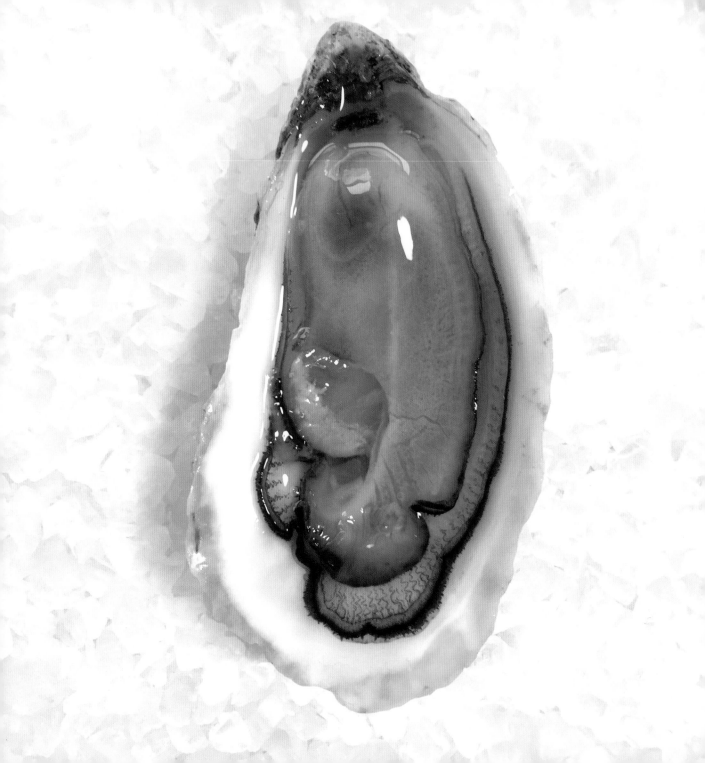

Moon Rise

CRASSOSTREA VIRGINICA

MERROIR A slender, skinny shell houses an oyster redolent of waterlogged florals and damp wood. The morsel is meaty, but not overly dense, layered with brine and creamy in texture. The bite ends with notes of simple syrup that hang around for just the right amount of time.

Cape Cod Bay, MA

TASTING PROFILE

BRINE	●●●
SWEETNESS	●●
MINERALITY	●
NOSE	●●●
FINISH	●●

TEXTURE

- ✓ MEATY
- ✓ SMOOTH
- ✓ TOOTHSOME
- ✓ TENDER
- ✓ CLEAN

SHELL SIZE

MEAT-TO-SHELL RATIO

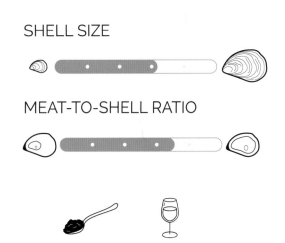

PEARL OF WISDOM All oysters pack a wallop of minerals like zinc and copper, but Atlantic oysters lead the way in this department. Pacific oysters also contain these minerals but at a much lower concentration. The result? The sweetness of the Pacifics comes through much easier than does the zing of many Atlantic oysters.

TRY IT WITH A macerated raspberry top. Pour a semi-sweet Riesling for a luscious pairing.

Moonstone

CRASSOSTREA VIRGINICA

MERROIR A very nice sized oyster whose aroma hints of seaweed and deep ocean. Sipping reveals an intense brine while the bite is robust with flavors of stone and spinach. The texture is light and lean. A long and full-flavored finish is rich with slate and soil before trailing off. Be sure to admire the shells; they look as if they could be moon rocks, with their ivory coloring and hints of copper.

Point Judith Pond
Narragansett, RI

TASTING PROFILE

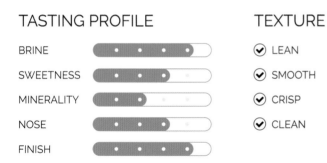

BRINE

SWEETNESS

MINERALITY

NOSE

FINISH

TEXTURE

✓ LEAN

✓ SMOOTH

✓ CRISP

✓ CLEAN

SHELL SIZE

MEAT-TO-SHELL RATIO

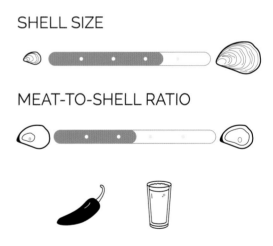

PEARL OF WISDOM Farmed oysters tend to live a good life. Protected from predators and thus without the need to fight for space, they tend to grow faster than wild oysters, who also have to filter more water, often filled with sand and mud, to get their vital nutrients.

TRY IT WITH A touch of jalapeño. Drink a German-style Kölsch brew.

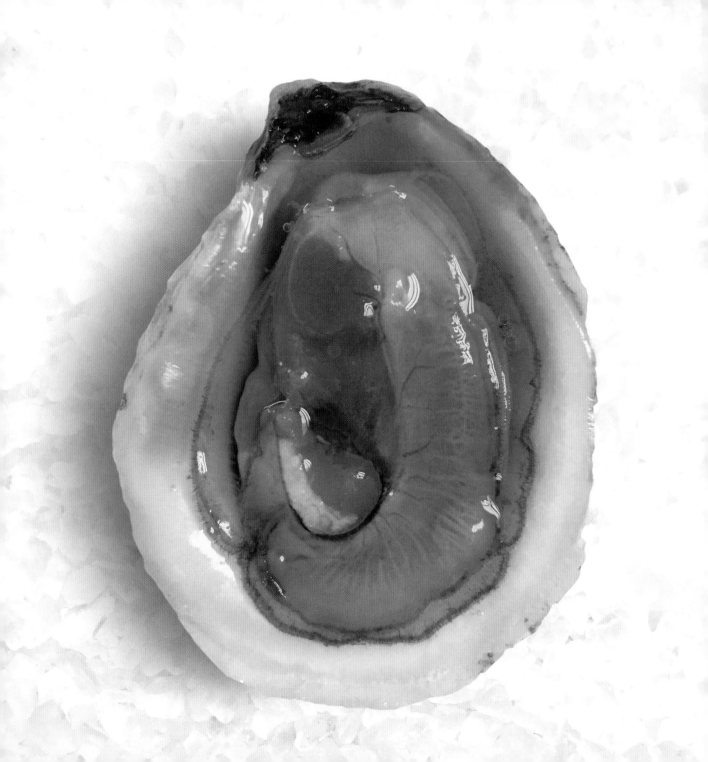

Murder Point

CRASSOSTREA VIRGINICA

MERROIR Another bright addition to the Gulf oyster scene, Murder Point oysters have a clean, elegant shell with hints of purple and green. An aroma of an early fog rolling over the bay piques the nostrils, with notes of sea grass and earth. The golden-cast meat is a wonderful hue, and it is tucked neatly around the shell. A sip of the crisp liquor reveals a salted butter note while a delightful chomp into the ample meat releases a creamy, fresh-churned butter savoriness. The finish rolls out with touches of metallic flavor and cream.

Portersville Bay, AL

TASTING PROFILE

BRINE	
SWEETNESS	
MINERALITY	
NOSE	
FINISH	

TEXTURE

- ✓ VELVETY
- ✓ BUTTERY
- ✓ MEATY
- ✓ SMOOTH
- ✓ CRISP

SHELL SIZE

MEAT-TO-SHELL RATIO

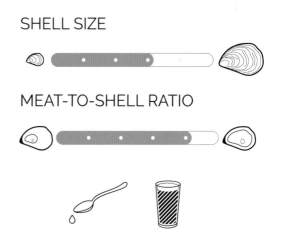

PEARL OF WISDOM In 1930, two oystermen who had leases on private oyster beds in the same area got in an argument. One shot the other over the rights to harvest the oysters, hence the name Murder Point.

TRY IT WITH A few drops of beer vinegar mignonette. Pair with a honey brown ale.

Nauti Pilgrim

CRASSOSTREA VIRGINICA

MERROIR The gorgeous ivory shells are tinged with a rich, green seaweed color. Inhale the aromatics of early-morning ocean air. The sublime ivory-colored meat has a paunchy belly glistening with liquor. The silky texture gives way to hints of green pepper and a burst of candy, finishing with hints of clean steel and a quickly fading brine.

Plymouth Bay, MA

TASTING PROFILE

BRINE

SWEETNESS

MINERALITY

NOSE

FINISH

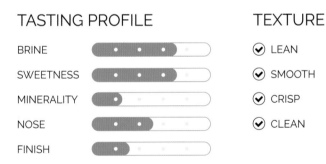

TEXTURE

- ✓ LEAN
- ✓ SMOOTH
- ✓ CRISP
- ✓ CLEAN

SHELL SIZE

MEAT-TO-SHELL RATIO

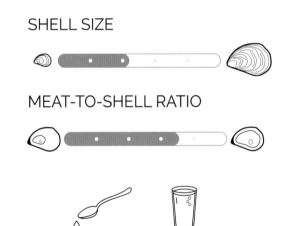

PEARL OF WISDOM Pilgrims and early settlers to New England learned from Native Americans about the abundance of oysters along the coastlines and in the bays. Knowing the various ways oysters can be prepared and eaten (raw, stewed, etc.) became vital to surviving the harsh winters.

TRY IT WITH A dab of cranberry sauce, to go classic Pilgrim. Try a dry and crisp cider to accompany it.

Nisqually Sweet

CRASSOSTREA GIGAS

MERROIR A drifting scent of fresh-cut watermelon on a summer's eve rolls over a deep-cupped, vibrant, ribboned shell. Tucked inside is a splendid ink-toned, edged meat, billowing and brimming with liquor. The sip is an indulgence in fresh, bright brine while the bite is rich with salted sweet cream and notes of stainless steel. Finishes crisp and light.

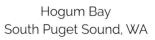

Hogum Bay
South Puget Sound, WA

TASTING PROFILE

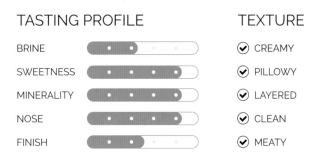

BRINE

SWEETNESS

MINERALITY

NOSE

FINISH

TEXTURE

- ✓ CREAMY
- ✓ PILLOWY
- ✓ LAYERED
- ✓ CLEAN
- ✓ MEATY

SHELL SIZE

MEAT-TO-SHELL RATIO

PEARL OF WISDOM The Nisqually River is fed by the streams and glacial melt of Mount Rainier, which provides a rich source of nutrients and minerals for the oysters. They are officially cultivated by the National Fish & Oyster Co., and although the company has grown oysters since 1939, they haven't done any commercial fishing since the 1950s.

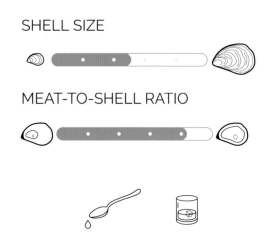

TRY IT WITH An apple-ginger mignonette. A sweet white Vermouth makes for a very elegant pairing.

Nonesuch

CRASSOSTREA VIRGINICA

MERROIR A deep emerald-hued shell twists and turns to reveal delightful scents of fog and silt. Peachy meat sprawls in a zinc-tinged liquor. A perfectly tender texture reveals robust earthen- and garden-fresh greens, mixed with the right amount of brine. Revel in an impeccable wash of lingering zing as the flavors dissipate like a wispy cloud.

Nonesuch Point
Scarborough, ME

TASTING PROFILE

BRINE

SWEETNESS

MINERALITY

NOSE

FINISH

TEXTURE

✓ BUTTERY

✓ TOOTHSOME

✓ MEATY

✓ CRISP

✓ SMOOTH

SHELL SIZE

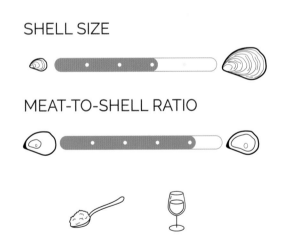

MEAT-TO-SHELL RATIO

PEARL OF WISDOM Abigail Carroll, owner of Nonesuch, says she "discovered ground seeding (of oysters) by accident. A friend dove at the site and emerged with incredible green oysters that had escaped from our gear and didn't look anything like what we were growing. I instantly fell in love with these oysters and began to ground seed."

TRY IT WITH A blood-orange granita topping. Pair with a racy Grüner Veltliner to add to all the luscious flavors.

Olympia

OSTREA LURIDA

MERROIR Inhale deeply a robust scent of zinc and copper. A quick sip of liquor reveals even more metallic notes. The petite meat is rich with earthiness and leather. With a smooth, glossy texture throughout, this oyster is great to roll around the tongue, to really soak in all the flavors. The brine kicks in late with hints of steamed-spinach. A long, lingering minerality finishes things off. The miniature slate-and-ivy colored shell has a stunning pearlescent glow on the interior, reminiscent of a 50-cent piece. A true delight.

Totten Inlet &
Hood Canal Region, WA

TASTING PROFILE

BRINE

SWEETNESS

MINERALITY

NOSE

FINISH

TEXTURE

- ✓ TENDER
- ✓ SILKY
- ✓ SMOOTH
- ✓ LAYERED
- ✓ ZINGY

SHELL SIZE

MEAT-TO-SHELL RATIO

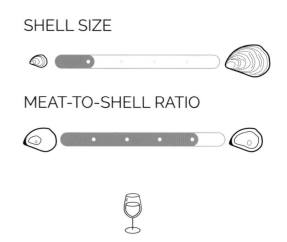

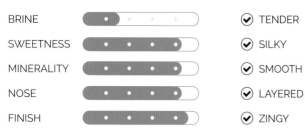

PEARL OF WISDOM Olympias, or Olys as they're nicknamed, are the only oysters native to the West Coast of North America and are so named after the particular region of the Puget Sound where they originate. They are also their own unique species of oyster, named Ostrea lurida.

TRY IT WITH Nada. This is one to enjoy without toppings. A Vinho Verde pairs well.

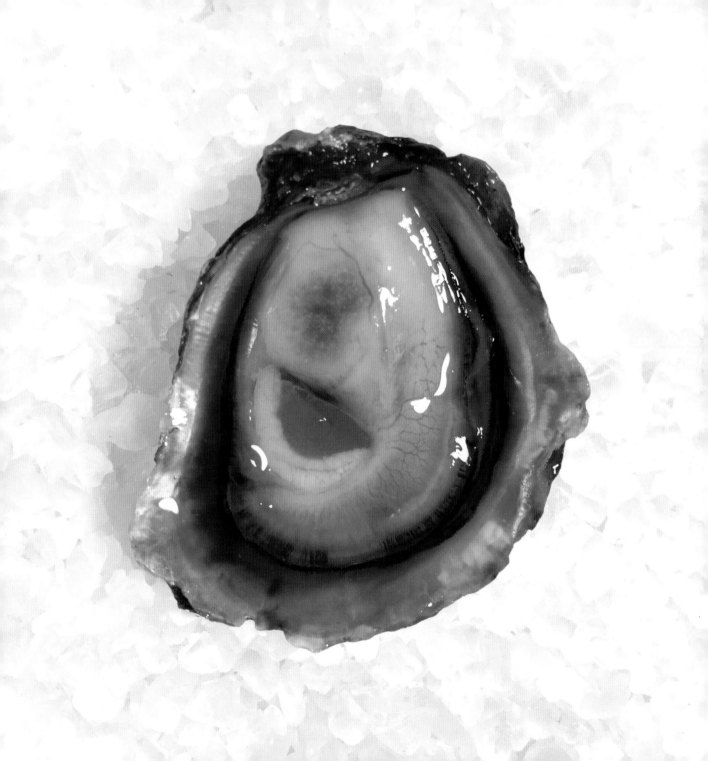

Osterville

CRASSOSTREA VIRGINICA

MERROIR A deep inhale reveals crisp ocean air full of floating salt. The clean, ivory meat is tucked into a wash of briny liquor. Hints of fresh greens and black pepper lie behind a robust first bite that stays salty all the way to the last bite. A whisper of sugar sneaks up at the finish. As you flip over the shell, take a look at the long, swooping teardrop shape with beautiful bronze-and-emerald striping.

West Bay—Osterville
Cape Cod, MA

TASTING PROFILE

BRINE

SWEETNESS

MINERALITY

NOSE

FINISH

TEXTURE

⊘ CRISP

⊘ CLEAN

⊘ SMOOTH

⊘ LEAN

⊘ BURSTING

SHELL SIZE

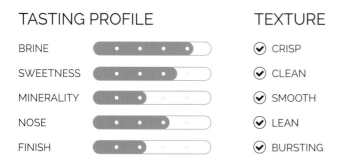

MEAT-TO-SHELL RATIO

PEARL OF WISDOM The name of this oyster sounds oyster-ish enough. Why? The first colonial settlers who arrived in the town in 1639 quickly learned the abundance of oysters around them. Its original name, Oyster Island Village, was shortened to Oysterville, and then, in 1815, the name was finally changed to Osterville after a town vote.

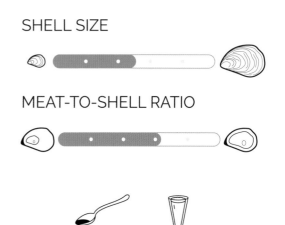

TRY IT WITH A roasted-tomato-and-basil mignonette. A Czech-style pilsner works nicely to wash it all down.

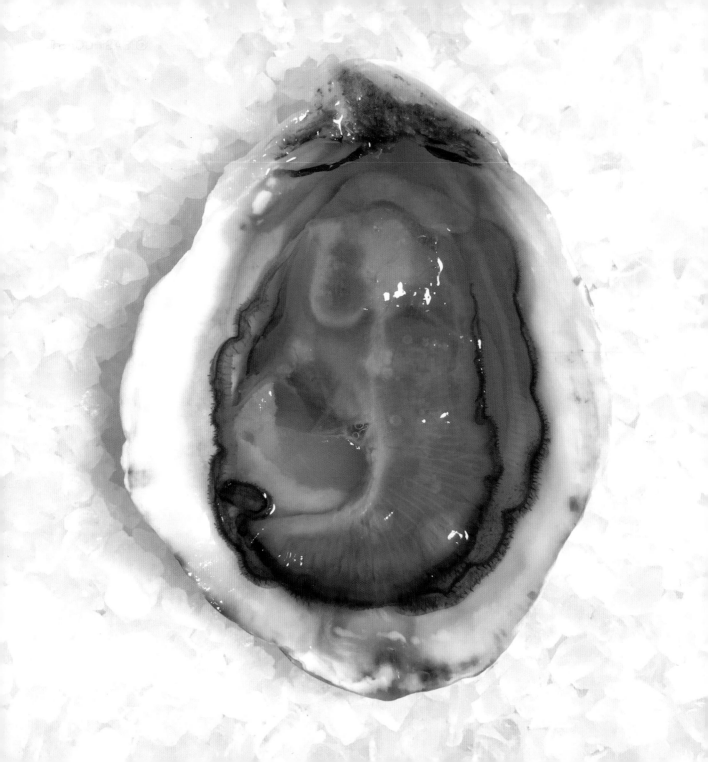

Oysterponds

CRASSOSTREA VIRGINICA

MERROIR The rich amber shell is layered with coal-dark colorings. The nose is a delightful mix of fog and sea mist. The liquor sip reveals full-bodied salty goodness. The rich flavor in these delectable oysters is full of intense brine and a savory metallic taste, while the texture is silky with a nice chew. A slow linger of brine and tin with pockets of simple syrup sprinkled in finishes things off.

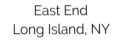

East End
Long Island, NY

TASTING PROFILE

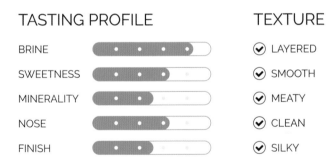

BRINE

SWEETNESS

MINERALITY

NOSE

FINISH

TEXTURE

- ✓ LAYERED
- ✓ SMOOTH
- ✓ MEATY
- ✓ CLEAN
- ✓ SILKY

SHELL SIZE

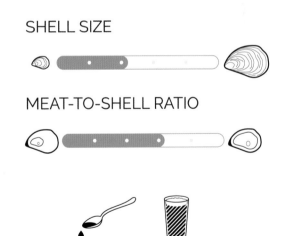

MEAT-TO-SHELL RATIO

PEARL OF WISDOM The Tuttle family, the owners, have had claim to the creek that is home to Oysterponds since the 1640s. The near-complete draining of the estuary from tidal flow circulates the water twice a day, creating a nutrient bonanza for the oysters to feed upon.

TRY IT WITH A beer mignonette drizzled over the top. A Märzen makes a great pairing.

Paine's Creek

CRASSOSTREA VIRGINICA

MERROIR A delicate aroma tinged with honeysuckle and honey greets the nose as you approach a Paine's Creek. The shell is a shiny, near-iridescent green and bronze color, offsetting the ivory-hued meat soaking in a mild brine liquor. These oysters make easy eating, being light and silky in texture, while the flavor has notes of broth and grass. A sweetness and subtle minerality rounds out the experience with finesse.

Brewster, MA

TASTING PROFILE

BRINE

SWEETNESS

MINERALITY

NOSE

FINISH

TEXTURE

- ✓ BURSTING
- ✓ SLIPPERY
- ✓ SNAPPY
- ✓ LEAN
- ✓ CRISP

SHELL SIZE

MEAT-TO-SHELL RATIO

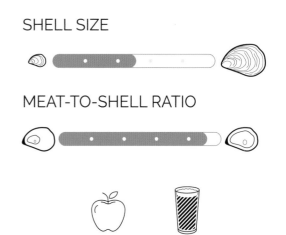

PEARL OF WISDOM You want pizza with your oysters? Paine's Creek owner Joey Werzanski's day job is running Joey's Pizzeria, the only pizzeria you're likely to find that also serves oysters.

TRY IT WITH Finely diced apples spread over the top. A crisp Maibock lager makes a good match.

Paradise

CRASSOSTREA GIGAS

MERROIR The aromatic, fresh and almost peppery scents of this delightful West Coast oyster waft delicately over feathery-edged meat. The liquor looks innocent enough, but it smacks with a super-intense brine hit that borders on overwhelming. The chunky meat has a gratifying bite with both subtle cream and black pepper flavors. Revel in the silky texture while the aftertaste lingers and fades.

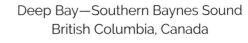

Deep Bay—Southern Baynes Sound
British Columbia, Canada

TASTING PROFILE

BRINE

SWEETNESS

MINERALITY

NOSE

FINISH

TEXTURE

- ✓ CREAMY
- ✓ MEATY
- ✓ SMOOTH
- ✓ TENDER
- ✓ LAYERED

SHELL SIZE

MEAT-TO-SHELL RATIO

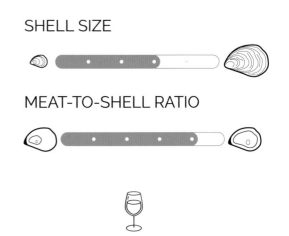

PEARL OF WISDOM Cindy Dekker & Ron Osmond run Paradise Oysters. Ron is out on the farm every day and Cindy oversees the processing facility. Together, they box and package oysters two days a week, which Ron considers his days off, because on those days he is away from the farm and can spend his day with Cindy.

TRY IT WITH Nothing. Skip the toppings, as these oysters are truly a rare treat. Pair with a lemony-tart Pinot Grigio.

Pemaquid

CRASSOSTREA VIRGINICA

MERROIR Deep brown-and-white shells reveal a nose that whispers of fog-soaked pine and wet moss. A massive copper start greets the tongue followed with a big brine flavor, smoothing into a zesty sweetness. The rich ivory meat is succulent, firm, and light. This is a taste of the Maine wilderness at its finest

Damariscotta River, ME

TASTING PROFILE

BRINE	●●●○
SWEETNESS	●●○
MINERALITY	●○
NOSE	●●○
FINISH	●○

TEXTURE

- ✓ SILKY
- ✓ LEAN
- ✓ ZESTY
- ✓ BURSTING
- ✓ TOOTHSOME

SHELL SIZE

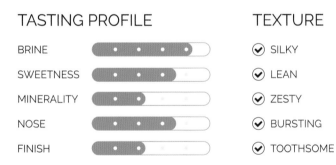

MEAT-TO-SHELL RATIO

PEARL OF WISDOM Maine has a unique coastline with its multitude of finger-like estuaries, formed by the glacial retreat of the last Ice Age. Many of these bays and inlets have very restricted openings to the sea, and their cold waters and undulating tides make for an ideal location for oysters to grow and thrive.

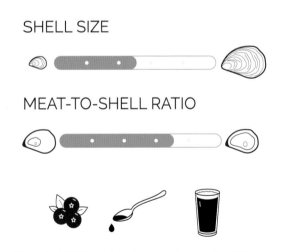

TRY IT WITH A blueberry mignonette. When in Maine, blueberries are a must. A fresh blueberry mignonette goes well with a frosty blueberry ale to wash it down.

Pickering Pass

CRASSOSTREA GIGAS

MERROIR The aromatic scent of cucumber greets the nose. Super-plump and portly meat nestles in the elongated, deep-cupped shell. The tasty liquor invites you to give the meat a hearty bite, revealing a resounding freshness and piquancy with undertones of steel. A creaminess rolls over the tongue and leads into a pleasantly long finish of grass and melon rind. Get a good look at the wavy candy-striped shell. Truly a beauty.

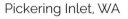

Pickering Inlet, WA

TASTING PROFILE

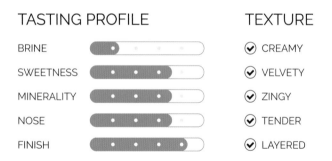

BRINE

SWEETNESS

MINERALITY

NOSE

FINISH

TEXTURE

✓ CREAMY

✓ VELVETY

✓ ZINGY

✓ TENDER

✓ LAYERED

SHELL SIZE

MEAT-TO-SHELL RATIO

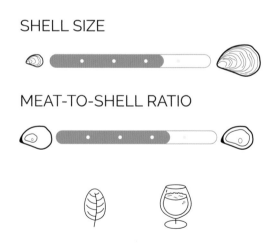

PEARL OF WISDOM The combination of water flow from the mouths of Hammersley, Totten, and Eld Inlet make this area a nutrient-rich buffet for rapid oyster growth. Charles Wilkes named it during the Wilkes Expedition of 1838–42, to honor Charles Pickering, one of the expedition's naturalists.

TRY IT WITH A basil leaf to garnish. Round out with a farmhouse ale.

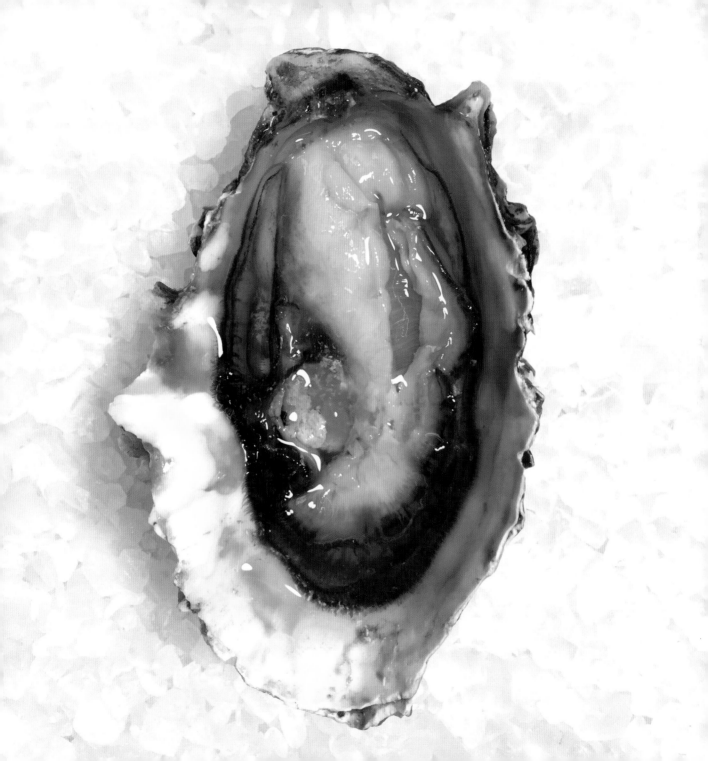

Plymouth Rock

CRASSOSTREA VIRGINICA

MERROIR These splendidly scalloped ivory shells are a classic example of an oyster home. The liquor has the potency you might experience when licking a gigantic salt block, or sucking on a bouillon cube. The meat is pleasantly dense, with a nice bite, and it has the essence of a rich broth. Hang on for a delightful finish that wanders through notes of brown sugar.

Plymouth, MA

TASTING PROFILE

BRINE	●●●●
SWEETNESS	●●●
MINERALITY	●
NOSE	●●●
FINISH	●●●

TEXTURE

- ✔ SNAPPY
- ✔ LEAN
- ✔ BUTTERY
- ✔ BURSTING
- ✔ CLEAN

SHELL SIZE

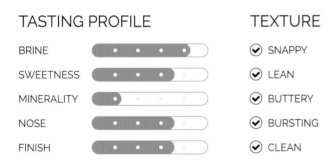

MEAT-TO-SHELL RATIO

PEARL OF WISDOM Yes, it's that Plymouth Rock. Oysters were a key staple of the diets of the Pilgrims, having been introduced to them by the Native Americans. Oysters were most likely eaten at the first Thanksgiving.

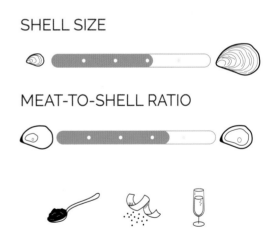

TRY IT WITH A fresh cranberry and orange zest mignonette. Pair with a sparkling white wine.

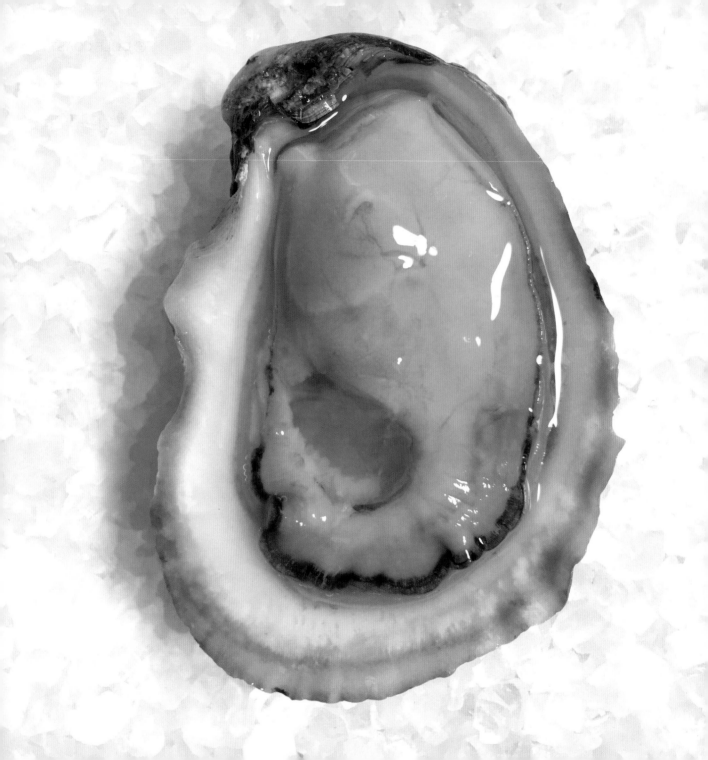

Point aux Pins

CRASSOSTREA VIRGINICA

MERROIR The scent of crisp summer morning along the bay with sweet notes of creamed spinach greets the senses first. Cozied up inside the shell is pristine, chubby meat gleaming with liquor. A sip is crisp and robust with hints of seagrass. The body is near flawless with delicate cilia edging. A silky bite is flavorful and light on the brine. A light finish fades sublimely and leaves one wanting more. A fine example of a Gulf oyster and what Grand Bay can provide.

Grand Bay, AL

TASTING PROFILE

BRINE
SWEETNESS
MINERALITY
NOSE
FINISH

TEXTURE

- ✓ SILKY
- ✓ BUTTERY
- ✓ MEATY
- ✓ CLEAN
- ✓ CRISP

SHELL SIZE

MEAT-TO-SHELL RATIO

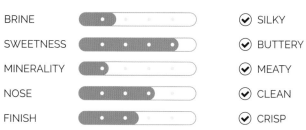

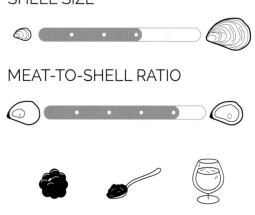

PEARL OF WISDOM Nurtured in the nutrient-rich waters of Grand Bay, Alabama, the Point aux Pins oyster begins life in the Auburn Shellfish Laboratory, where native Cedar Point, Alabama, oysters are induced to spawn in the spring of the year. When the spat have set on microculch (tiny pieces of oyster shell) and are large enough, farmers move them to the Point aux Pins site on Grand Bay, where they mature for harvest.

TRY IT WITH A daub of blackberry jam. Pair with a local Gose beer.

Puffer's Petite

CRASSOSTREA VIRGINICA

MERROIR A hefty shell with vibrant emerald and chocolate tones cradles a bounty of meat and liquor. A fragrant sea spray aroma swirls over the pleasantly plump bivalve. A quick sip of the liquor reveals a delightful brine kick, while the texture is smooth and bouncy. The supremely earthy flavor is balanced with a delicate, almost honey-like sweetness. The well-balanced finish dawdles long enough to make you crave another.

Mayo Beach
Wellfleet, MA

TASTING PROFILE

BRINE	●●●●○
SWEETNESS	●●●○
MINERALITY	●○○○
NOSE	●●●○
FINISH	●●○○

TEXTURE

- ✓ LEAN
- ✓ SMOOTH
- ✓ CRISP
- ✓ CLEAN

SHELL SIZE

MEAT-TO-SHELL RATIO

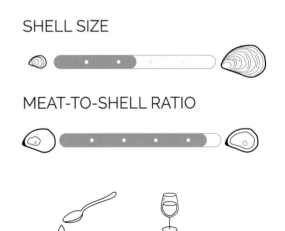

PEARL OF WISDOM The oyster is named after its grower. This family team farms the oysters locally on the tidal flats of Mayo Beach in Massachusetts. The daily tidal exchange of 12 feet means the Puffers only have about three hours to work before high tide starts.

TRY IT WITH A drop of simple mignonette. Sip a Manzanilla sherry to further enhance the flavors.

Quonnie Rock

CRASSOSTREA VIRGINICA

MERROIR The delicate nose is reminiscent of a frost-tinged morning near the ocean. The bulbous shell is brimming with liquor and purple-hued meat that is clean and uniform. Biting through the smooth and glossy texture reveals an eye-popping dose of brine that carries right through the finish, almost overwhelming the subtle flavors of mushroom and butter along the way.

Quonochontaug Pond
Charlestown, RI

TASTING PROFILE

BRINE

SWEETNESS

MINERALITY

NOSE

FINISH

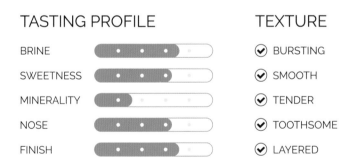

TEXTURE

- ✓ BURSTING
- ✓ SMOOTH
- ✓ TENDER
- ✓ TOOTHSOME
- ✓ LAYERED

SHELL SIZE

MEAT-TO-SHELL RATIO

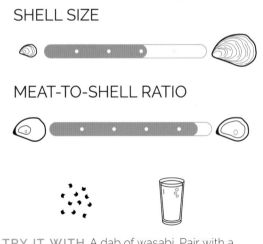

PEARL OF WISDOM Oyster farms help improve the quality of the oceans and bays they occupy because the oysters feed on particulate matter and nutrients that might otherwise cloud waterways. The cleaner water allows for more light to pass through, allowing plankton, seaweed, and other food to grow and the local ecosystem to flourish.

TRY IT WITH A dab of wasabi. Pair with a sparkling, dry cider.

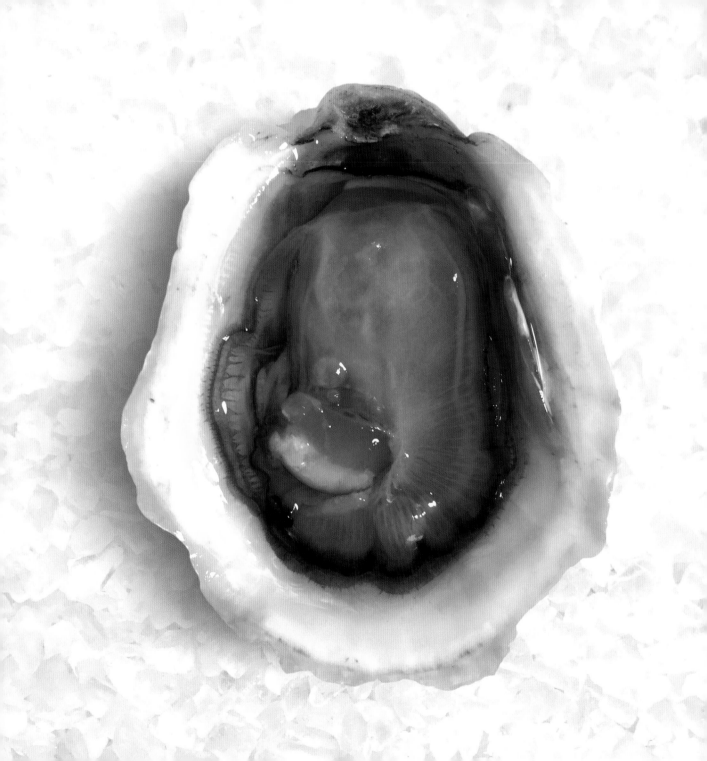

Race Point

CRASSOSTREA VIRGINICA

MERROIR Beware the immediate brine punch, zesty with hints of green pepper, steel, and sugar. There is a lingering saltiness on the finish that only hangs around long enough to crave another bite. The gorgeous oval shell, patterned with zebra-striping, is worth admiring as you order another round.

Provincetown, MA

TASTING PROFILE

BRINE

SWEETNESS

MINERALITY

NOSE

FINISH

TEXTURE

- ✓ ZESTY
- ✓ ZINGY
- ✓ SNAPPY
- ✓ BURSTING
- ✓ SILKY

SHELL SIZE

MEAT-TO-SHELL RATIO

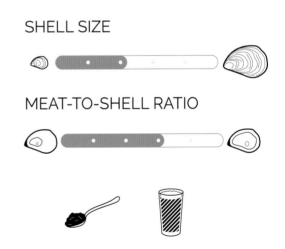

PEARL OF WISDOM An oyster's shell is formed layer-by-layer from the inside by a liquid called nacre. Each layer is about as thin as a layer of tissue paper.

TRY IT WITH A dab of apricot jam. To further enhance the flavor, pair with an apricot ale.

Riptide

CRASSOSTREA VIRGINICA

MERROIR Kick back and take in the light sea breeze scent of these oysters. The flaxen-hued meat brims to the edges of the shell with plenty of brine, with peeks of simple-syrup in the liquor. A silky and robust bite reveals a delightful metallic tone and hints of buttery goodness. The finish is lightning-fast, with continued satisfying hits of very smooth minerals.

Westport, MA

TASTING PROFILE

BRINE

SWEETNESS

MINERALITY

NOSE

FINISH

TEXTURE

✓ SILKY

✓ LEAN

✓ BURSTING

✓ CRISP

✓ CLEAN

SHELL SIZE

MEAT-TO-SHELL RATIO

PEARL OF WISDOM Riptides are so named because they grow in the energetic Westport River, located between Narragansett and Buzzards Bay in Massachusetts.

TRY IT WITH A touch of beet relish and a pinch of dill. A flute of Cava makes for a perfect pairing.

Royal Miyagi

CRASSOSTREA GIGAS

MERROIR The first thing you notice after the pretty blue and purple striped shells is the fragrant aroma of watermelon Bubblicious bubble gum. Cradled inside and swathed in a luscious liquor is a dense but pillowy meat. Hints of cream seep through a velvety texture. The finish is highlighted with a wondrous, slightly salted kiwi that fades like a summer sunset.

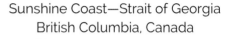

Sunshine Coast—Strait of Georgia
British Columbia, Canada

TASTING PROFILE

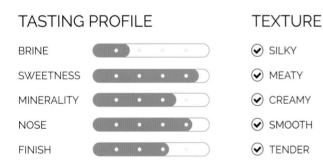

BRINE	
SWEETNESS	
MINERALITY	
NOSE	
FINISH	

TEXTURE

- ✓ SILKY
- ✓ MEATY
- ✓ CREAMY
- ✓ SMOOTH
- ✓ TENDER

SHELL SIZE

MEAT-TO-SHELL RATIO

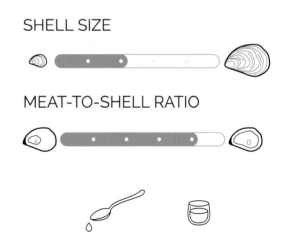

PEARL OF WISDOM How fast is fast shucking? A well-experienced shucker can speed through 4,000 to 6,000 oysters every day.

TRY IT WITH An herbaceous mignonette. Pair with a Junmai Daiginjo sake.

Salt Nugget

CRASSOSTREA GIGAS

MERROIR Like a rolling wave, the shell ripples with glimmers of white and green. A fragrant nose of steamed spinach accompanies the extremely plump meat tucked into the shell. The dark-tinted edging of the meat is beautiful to behold. The brine of the bite transitions into a blanket of salt and cucumber to make a delectable finish.

Western Shores
Hood Canal, WA

TASTING PROFILE

BRINE	
SWEETNESS	
MINERALITY	
NOSE	
FINISH	

TEXTURE

- ✓ ZINGY
- ✓ SILKY
- ✓ DENSE
- ✓ MEATY
- ✓ TOOTHSOME

SHELL SIZE

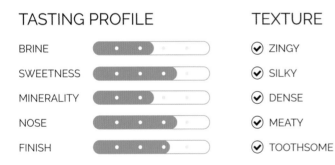

MEAT-TO-SHELL RATIO

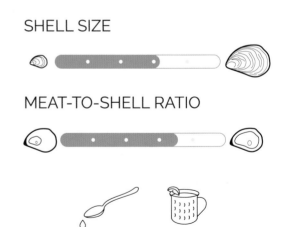

TRY IT WITH A carrot-ginger mignonette. A Moscow Mule is a punchy partner.

PEARL OF WISDOM Oysters have been around for fifteen million years, and in some places their shell deposits are 50 feet thick.

Shibumi

CRASSOSTREA VIRGINICA

MERROIR An enormously fragrant melon aroma wafts from the brown, purple, and white-striped shell. The liquor is laced with a subtle sweetness, tinged with metallic notes. The meat is firm with a delightful crunch hinted with cream and cucumber, while the finish is crisp with a balanced brine.

Eld Inlet
Puget Sound, WA

TASTING PROFILE

BRINE

SWEETNESS

MINERALITY

NOSE

FINISH

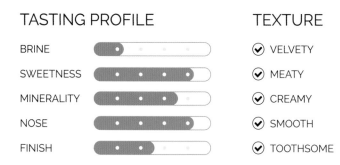

TEXTURE

- ✔ VELVETY
- ✔ MEATY
- ✔ CREAMY
- ✔ SMOOTH
- ✔ TOOTHSOME

SHELL SIZE

MEAT-TO-SHELL RATIO

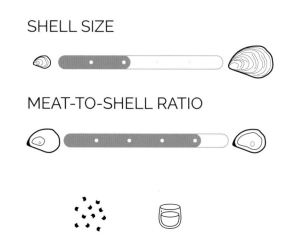

PEARL OF WISDOM Super-tumbled oysters like Shibumis typically have ultra-smooth shells. Not only are stronger shells prettier, but the meat will be plumper. Tumbling, which involves putting the oysters through a giant rolling canister every month or so, lengthens the maturation period, allowing flavors to develop more fully.

TRY IT WITH A sprinkle of parsley or dill. A nigori sake makes for a memorable pairing.

Shigoku

CRASSOSTREA GIGAS

MERROIR Behold the exotic bronze rippled shell. The perfume from this oyster is unmistakable. A nice brine kick sneaks up amongst the intense slate and melon as you savor the velvety texture. Relish the slow fade of those flavors on the finish. A scrumptious treat of an oyster.

Willapa Bay & Samish Bay, WA

TASTING PROFILE

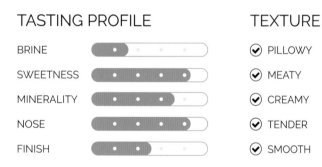

BRINE

SWEETNESS

MINERALITY

NOSE

FINISH

TEXTURE

- ✓ PILLOWY
- ✓ MEATY
- ✓ CREAMY
- ✓ TENDER
- ✓ SMOOTH

SHELL SIZE

MEAT-TO-SHELL RATIO

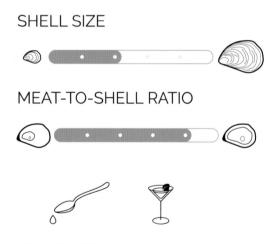

PEARL OF WISDOM Shigoku means "ultimate" in Japanese. And they are crafted as such, tumbling naturally twice a day with the tides in bags to create their lavish, deep shells.

TRY IT WITH A herby mignonette. Sip a basil gin martini.

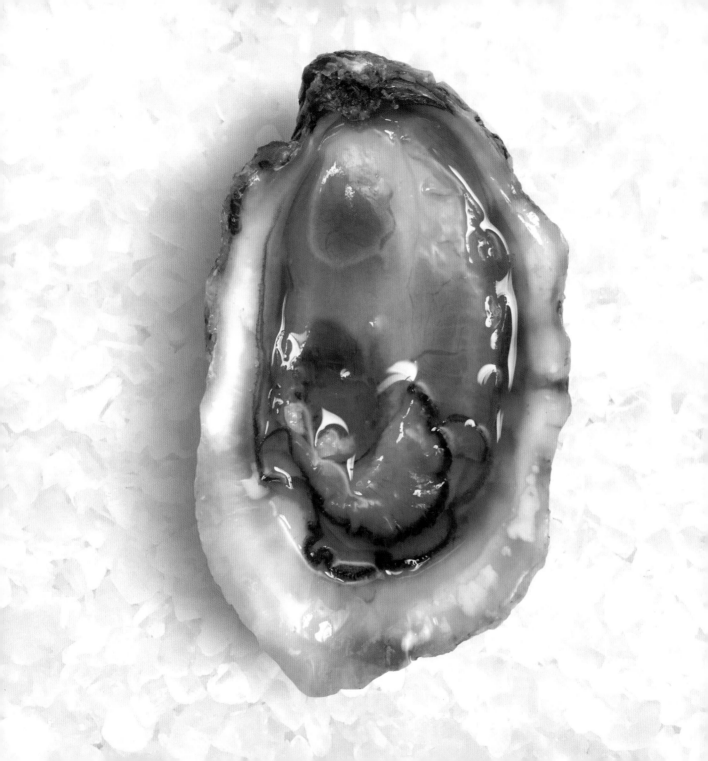

Ship Shoal

CRASSOSTREA VIRGINICA

MERROIR The aroma of this oyster is a fresh, wet ocean mist with a subtle suggestion of florals. Plump meat fills the shell, surrounded by lots of light, mild liquor. Hints of woodland and damp soil with a soft linger of moss and silt accompany the copious brine. Take notice of the shells that carry a weather-beaten look characteristic of the tidal grooves of the Chesapeake Bay where they're farmed.

Magotha Bay, VA

TASTING PROFILE

BRINE	●●●○
SWEETNESS	●●○
MINERALITY	●○
NOSE	●●○
FINISH	●○

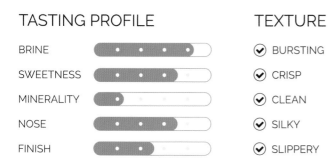

TEXTURE

- ✓ BURSTING
- ✓ CRISP
- ✓ CLEAN
- ✓ SILKY
- ✓ SLIPPERY

SHELL SIZE

MEAT-TO-SHELL RATIO

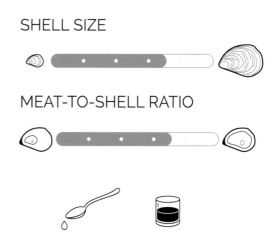

PEARL OF WISDOM Unlike most Chesapeake Bay oysters, these get much of their wonderful brine flavoring from a mix of the Occohannock Creek and the Magothy Bay waters where they sit.

TRY IT WITH A smoky mignonette. Sip an aromatic peat whiskey.

Stingray

CRASSOSTREA VIRGINICA

MERROIR Despite the name, there's no sting to fear here. The chocolate-hued shell is supremely slurp friendly. A simple seagrass salt scent drifts over the liquor lacquered interior. This classic Chesapeake Bay oyster has decidedly plump and sweet meat with a solid hit of brininess. The finish is deliciously terse, with a slight metallic essence that floats on the taste buds.

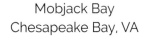

Mobjack Bay
Chesapeake Bay, VA

TASTING PROFILE

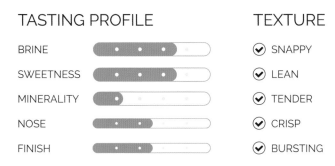

BRINE

SWEETNESS

MINERALITY

NOSE

FINISH

TEXTURE

✓ SNAPPY

✓ LEAN

✓ TENDER

✓ CRISP

✓ BURSTING

SHELL SIZE

MEAT-TO-SHELL RATIO

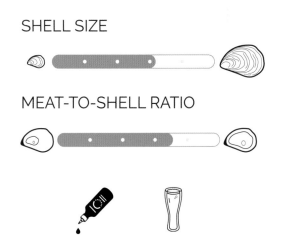

PEARL OF WISDOM Stingrays are so named for the bay oyster's chief predator, but the rack and bag cultivation method used to grow these oysters ultimately protects them.

TRY IT WITH A smidgen of Sriracha. Cool your palate with a Bohemian-style pilsner.

Sun Hollow

CRASSOSTREA GIGAS

MERROIR The meat inside these vibrant, striped shells is long and slender, bathing in lots of salted liquor. Take a deep sniff of a delightful lobster bisque aroma, layered with buttery salts. The first bite is a wonderful kick of brine with hints of chowder creaminess, then a rollout of iron and fruitiness. The texture is silky and worth savoring.

Southwestern Inlets
Hood Canal, WA

TASTING PROFILE

BRINE	
SWEETNESS	
MINERALITY	
NOSE	
FINISH	

TEXTURE

- ✔ LAYERED
- ✔ CREAMY
- ✔ SILKY
- ✔ ZINGY
- ✔ MEATY

PEARL OF WISDOM Sun Hollow oysters are beach bums. They are cultured on the beach, fighting the tides. This makes them clamp shut tightly during the exposure of low tides, preserving their liquor and freshness, and also making them a bit tougher to shuck.

SHELL SIZE

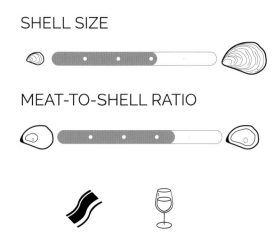

MEAT-TO-SHELL RATIO

TRY IT WITH A speck of Speck on top. Pair with a lightly oaked Chardonnay.

Sunken Meadow Gem

CRASSOSTREA VIRGINICA

MERROIR A lovely caramel-striped shell cradles a plump body inside, with a scent of salted broth. The liquor hints at chicken soup as it rolls across the palate. Dense meat provides a smooth texture with a lean bite, while the robust flavor starts mellow and flows into those poultry provisions that linger through the finish.

Dartmouth, MA

TASTING PROFILE

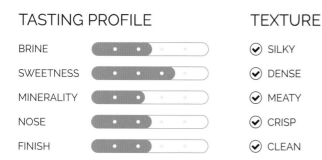

BRINE

SWEETNESS

MINERALITY

NOSE

FINISH

TEXTURE

- ✓ SILKY
- ✓ DENSE
- ✓ MEATY
- ✓ CRISP
- ✓ CLEAN

SHELL SIZE

MEAT-TO-SHELL RATIO

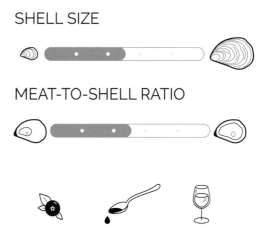

PEARL OF WISDOM Since all the sugars of an oyster are in the meat, you should always bite into an oyster. If you swallow, you're losing a lot of great flavor!

TRY IT WITH An elderberry-blossom mignonette, or just the berry itself. Pair with mead.

Sweet Jesus

CRASSOSTREA VIRGINICA

MERROIR The shell is stark white and weathered, with tones of silt and slate layered in. A rich aroma of eelgrass and the morning mist over Chesapeake Bay greets the nose. Golden meat is snuggled into the shell and needs a good chomp. The liquor is bountiful with subtle saltwater sweetness, while the meat is mild with tastes of tall grass and a unique earthiness that lingers on the finish. Definitely worth yelling "Sweet Jesus!" when you flip the cup.

Patuxent River—Chesapeake Bay
Hollywood, MD

TASTING PROFILE

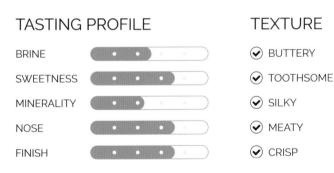

BRINE

SWEETNESS

MINERALITY

NOSE

FINISH

TEXTURE

- ✓ BUTTERY
- ✓ TOOTHSOME
- ✓ SILKY
- ✓ MEATY
- ✓ CRISP

SHELL SIZE

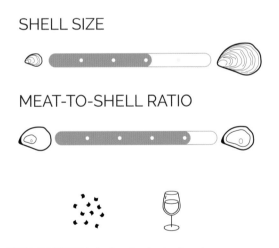

MEAT-TO-SHELL RATIO

PEARL OF WISDOM St. Mary's County Maryland, where the Sweet Jesus oyster hails from, is home of the U.S. National Oyster Shucking Contest and the U.S. National Oyster Cook-Off.

TRY IT WITH A simple dash of red pepper flakes. Pair with a crisp Pinot Blanc.

Totten Inlet Virginica

CRASSOSTREA VIRGINICA

MERROIR Delight in the scent of river meeting sea. Ample liquor hints of mild brine with a soft metallic flavor and underlying hints of simple syrup. The meat has a lovely hue that is very evenly textured and generously fills the cup. The bite is luscious and silky with a wonderful crispness. Subdued notes of earth, mushroom, and nuts float over the palate. While the finish is briny, it doesn't overstay its welcome. Check out the wonderfully textured shells colored with rich hues of blue and green.

Totten Inlet
South Puget Sound, WA

TASTING PROFILE

BRINE	
SWEETNESS	
MINERALITY	
NOSE	
FINISH	

TEXTURE

- ✓ PILLOWY
- ✓ BUTTERY
- ✓ TOOTHSOME
- ✓ BURSTING
- ✓ CRISP

SHELL SIZE

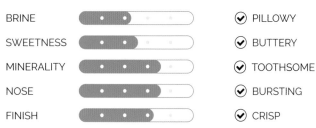

MEAT-TO-SHELL RATIO

PEARL OF WISDOM Totten Virginicas are the only Virginica species grown on the West Coast. They are also the first Eastern oyster grown commercially in Washington since 1900–20, when a large quantity was grown in Willapa Bay for the oyster-hungry San Francisco market, recognized for their superior flavor.

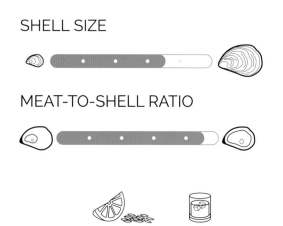

TRY IT WITH A tangy pop of Pomelo pulp. Add a piquant Paloma for a prime cocktail pairing.

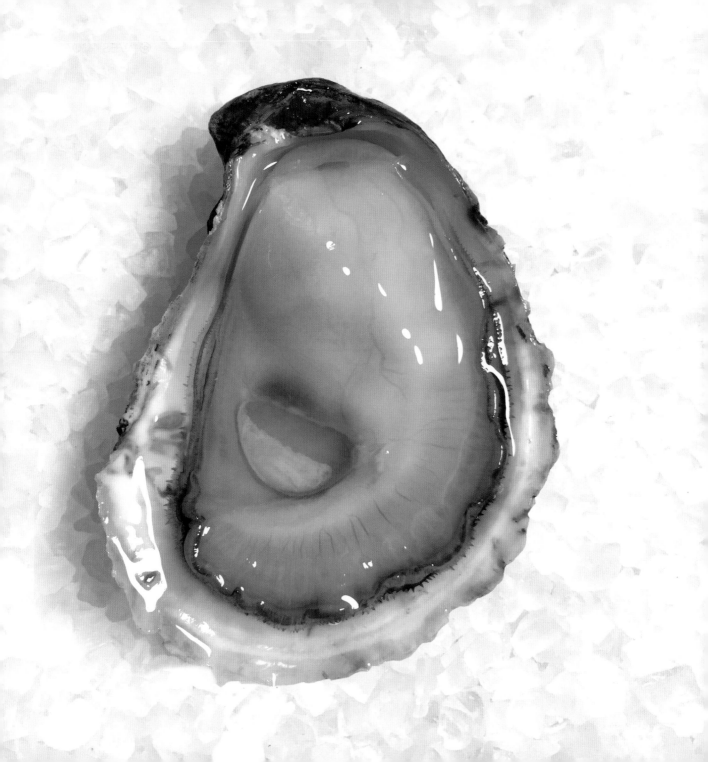

Totten Pacific

CRASSOSTREA GIGAS

MERROIR The rich blend of colors on this ruffled shell includes rose and lavender. Take a breath and smell the fragrant perfume of sea-spray-covered cantaloupe. Inside, behold a stout creamy meat soaking in its tasty liquor. A great big bite will reveal a nice crunch and an underlying creaminess. Flavors of watermelon and honeydew rind sprinkled with tin and steel peek through. The delightful finish lingers with cream and metallic notes.

Totten Inlet
South Puget Sound, WA

TASTING PROFILE

BRINE

SWEETNESS

MINERALITY

NOSE

FINISH

TEXTURE

- ✓ CREAMY
- ✓ DENSE
- ✓ CRUNCHY
- ✓ LAYERED
- ✓ ZINGY

SHELL SIZE

MEAT-TO-SHELL RATIO

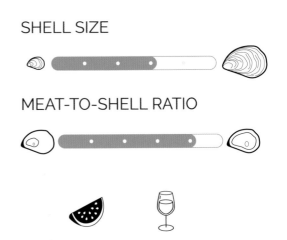

PEARL OF WISDOM Totten Inlet Oysters are raised in the same area as the Totten Virginica Oysters, but they are two different species and have different flavor profiles.

TRY IT WITH A dab of pickled watermelon rind on top. Pair with a fruit-forward Sancerre with vibrant acidity.

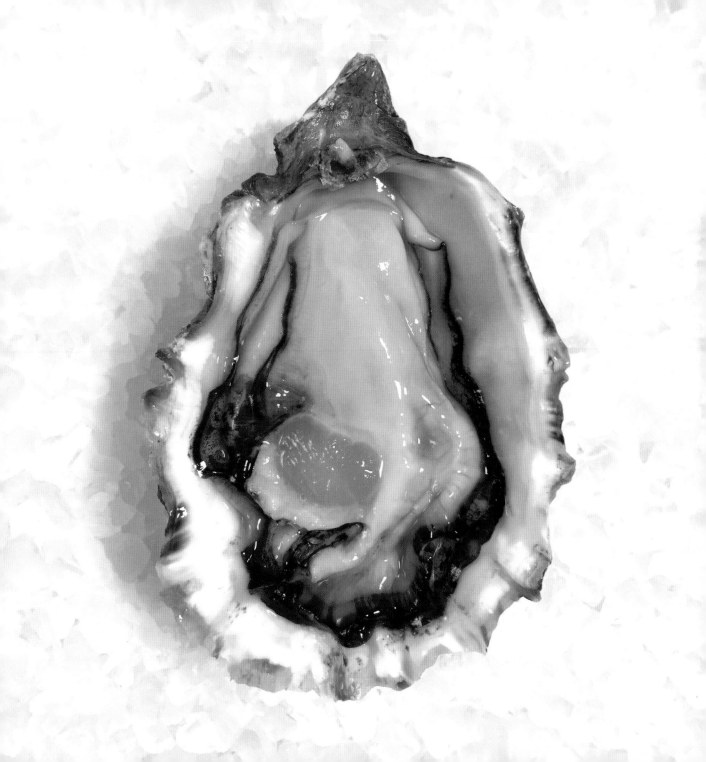

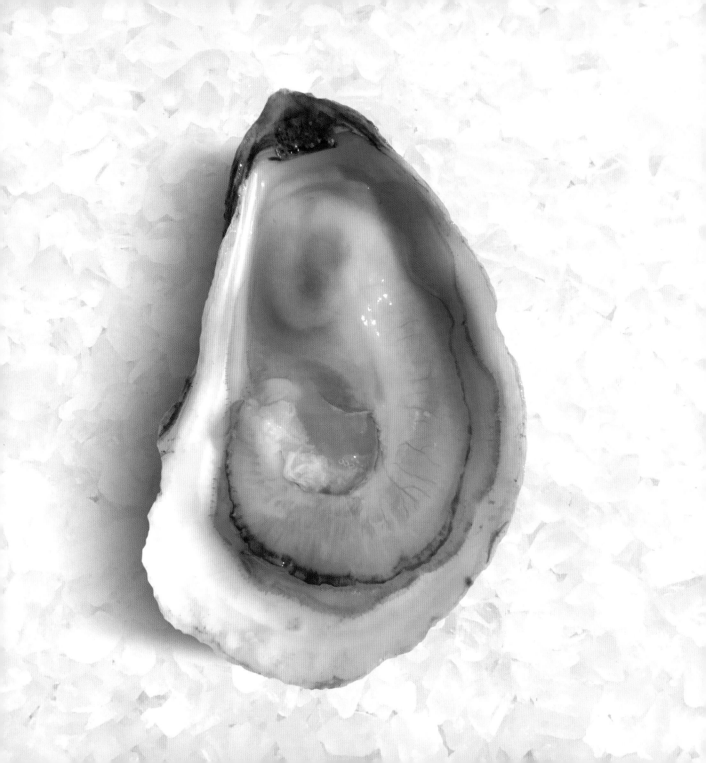

Wellfleet

CRASSOSTREA VIRGINICA

MERROIR The mixed gold and chocolate color of the shell is a delightful spectacle. A bright sea mist fragrance full of salts tickles the nose on the first sniff. The taste packs a surprisingly salty kick, with muted notes of damp earth and hearty charcuterie that blend wonderfully together. The meaty texture has a lean, yet firm bite with a refreshingly clean and crisp finish.

Wellfleet Harbor
Cape Cod Bay, MA

TASTING PROFILE

BRINE

SWEETNESS

MINERALITY

NOSE

FINISH

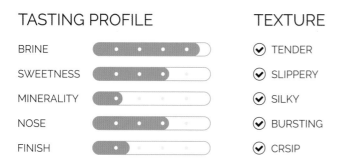

TEXTURE

- ✓ TENDER
- ✓ SLIPPERY
- ✓ SILKY
- ✓ BURSTING
- ✓ CRSIP

SHELL SIZE

MEAT-TO-SHELL RATIO

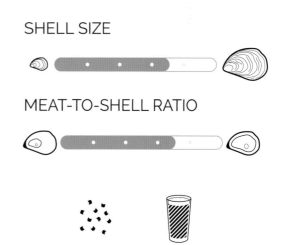

PEARL OF WISDOM In 1605, the French explorer Samuel de Champlain was so taken with the vivacity of the oyster population in the Wellfleet region, he named it "Port Aux Huitres." In the early 1800s, Wellfleet's native oyster population was nearly decimated due to a combination of plague and overfishing. Aquaculture, as we know it today, began with the replenishing of Wellfleet oysters.

TRY IT WITH A sprinkle of crumbled bacon or pork rinds over the top. Pair with a savory amber ale to augment the caramel notes.

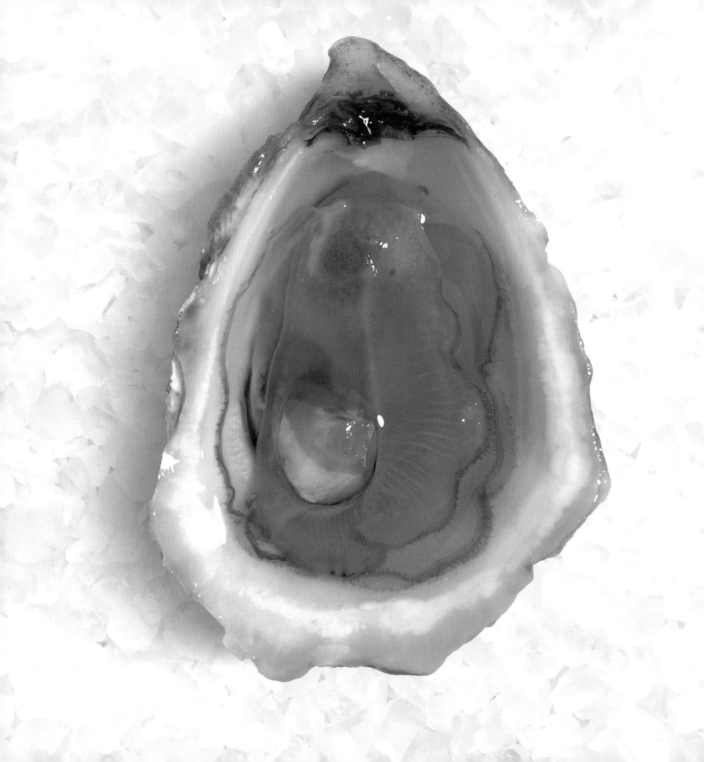

Whitecap

CRASSOSTREA VIRGINICA

MERROIR A refreshing, crisp scent of salt runs across the nose. Stashed away in the bronze and emerald shell is a delightful buttercream meat that nearly glows. Immersed in a gently brined liquor, the bite is very lean, but it packs a surprising punch of saltiness with earthy nuances. A crisp finish with hints of simple syrup fades quickly.

East Dennis
Cape Cod Bay, MA

TASTING PROFILE

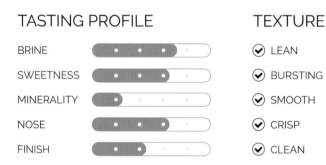

BRINE

SWEETNESS

MINERALITY

NOSE

FINISH

TEXTURE

⊘ LEAN

⊘ BURSTING

⊘ SMOOTH

⊘ CRISP

⊘ CLEAN

SHELL SIZE

MEAT-TO-SHELL RATIO

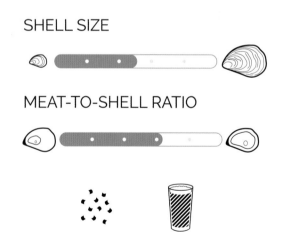

PEARL OF WISDOM The verb *to shuck* was first recorded in 1881. *Aww shucks* was first used around 1847.

TRY IT WITH A sprinkle of chili pepper flakes. Pair with an amber ale.

Wicked Pissah

CRASSOSTREA VIRGINICA

MERROIR A golden, tiger-striped shell opens to a fragrant yet light scent of seagrass. The meat fills the shell nicely, immersed in a subtle sweet liquid. While these oysters make for lean and easy eating, be ready for a sublime sweetness hidden in the brine that kicks in nicely and fades gently through the finish.

Cherrystone River
Chesapeake Bay, VA

TASTING PROFILE

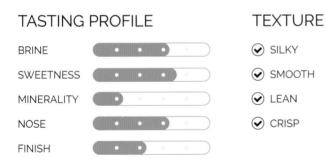

BRINE

SWEETNESS

MINERALITY

NOSE

FINISH

TEXTURE

✓ SILKY

✓ SMOOTH

✓ LEAN

✓ CRISP

SHELL SIZE

MEAT-TO-SHELL RATIO

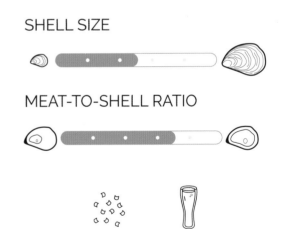

PEARL OF WISDOM Harvested and tagged exclusively for Ford's Fish Shack, these are grown and harvested in the Cherrystone River, on the lower eastern shore of the Chesapeake Bay, VA, now known as part of the Virginia Oyster Trail. Approximately 17,000 oysters are sold each month, with delivery to the restaurant within 24 hours of harvest. Fresh!

TRY IT WITH A smidge of grated fresh horseradish. Wash it down with a Czech-style pilsner.

Widow's Hole

CRASSOSTREA VIRGINICA

MERROIR The dark, rich chocolate and caramel colors are reminiscent of candy. The aroma suggests dried seaweed on a foggy summer morning. The meat is decidedly fleshy, with lots of liquor that overflows the shells. The body has a wonderful big bite with a crisp crunch that reveals a delightful sugariness encompassed by tin and metallics on the liquor. The finish lingers with delectable brine and mineral flavors

Greenport Harbor, NY

TASTING PROFILE

BRINE

SWEETNESS

MINERALITY

NOSE

FINISH

TEXTURE

⊘ TOOTHSOME

⊘ MEATY

⊘ VELVETY

⊘ BUTTERY

⊘ CRISP

SHELL SIZE

MEAT-TO-SHELL RATIO

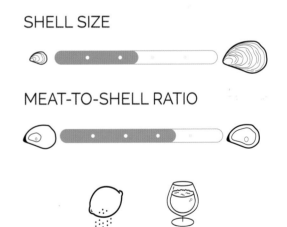

TRY IT WITH Lime zest and a pinch of lemon. Pour a summer session beer to enjoy.

PEARL OF WISDOM Michael and Isabel Osinski recall their start as oyster farmers. "My wife and I discovered, three years after buying it [our summer house] and two years after selling our software company [in 2001], that we owned 5 acres of bottom adjoining my beach. We knew that Greenport had been the oyster capital of New York and that no one was growing oysters here 15 years ago. So we got some permits and enslaved ourselves [farming oysters]."

Wildcat Cove

CRASSOSTREA GIGAS

MERROIR Get a whiff of freshly sliced melon before sipping the overflowing liquor, delicate with brine. A firm chomp on the rotund meat releases notes of cream and zinc in a silky, smooth texture. Expect hints of melon and sweet steamed vegetables on the finish that carry on for a good while. Admire the beautiful, deep-fluted shell, vibrant with bronze, purple, and emerald coloring.

South Puget Sound, WA

TASTING PROFILE

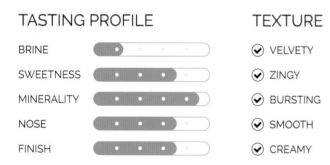

BRINE

SWEETNESS

MINERALITY

NOSE

FINISH

TEXTURE

- ✓ VELVETY
- ✓ ZINGY
- ✓ BURSTING
- ✓ SMOOTH
- ✓ CREAMY

SHELL SIZE

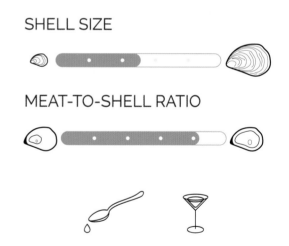

MEAT-TO-SHELL RATIO

PEARL OF WISDOM An adult oyster, while eating, can filter 30 gallons of water or more per day. Multiply this by the number of oysters in an oyster reef and you get an amount of algae cleaned from the water that would have a profound effect on the marine environment.

TRY IT WITH A few drops of gin on top. Sip a martini.

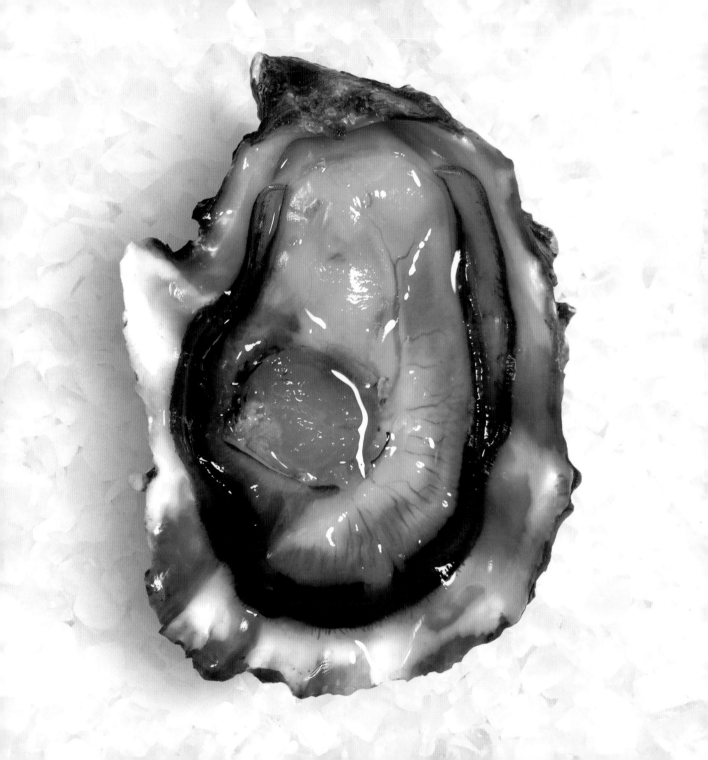

Wolf Beach

CRASSOSTREA GIGAS

MERROIR This oyster looks like something that stepped out of the Flintstones. Heavily barnacled and deep emerald shells could pass for dinosaur feet. Inhale a breezy, light melon scent. The asymmetrical shells house plump meats. A sip of the liquor reveals delicate brine. A stout bite is extremely mild and mellow in flavor; for a West Coast oyster, this taste is more reminiscent of a Gulf Coast. The finish is very light, with subtle hints of melon rind and cream.

Totten Inlent, WA

TASTING PROFILE

BRINE	
SWEETNESS	
MINERALITY	
NOSE	
FINISH	

TEXTURE

- ✓ CREAMY
- ✓ TENDER
- ✓ SILKY
- ✓ VELVETY
- ✓ SMOOTH

SHELL SIZE

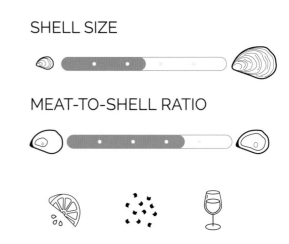

MEAT-TO-SHELL RATIO

PEARL OF WISDOM Oysters are among the only living creatures to grow asymmetrically, meaning their top and bottom shells are not mirror images of each other.

TRY IT WITH A sprinkle of dried seaweed flakes to enhance the nautical experience. Sip a Sauvignon Blanc.

CONCLUSION

SO MANY OYSTERS. SO LITTLE TIME.

"As I ate the oysters with their strong taste of the sea and their faint metallic taste that the cold white wine washed away, leaving only the sea taste and the succulent texture, and as I drank their cold liquid from each shell and washed it down with the crisp taste of the wine, I lost the empty feeling and began to be happy and to make plans."

—*Ernest Hemingway*, A Moveable Feast

The beauty of crafting oysters is that there is continual learning, tweaking, and adjusting by the farmers. A master brewer or wine-maker follows a similar process to find their perfect recipe. A slight variation in maintenance of the oysters, how often they're tumbled, or the movement of location of the oysters by just yards can have an effect on the overall taste and appearance of the product. Granted, an oyster's flavor can change daily, even hourly, based on the water around it. But even this allows for more addition into the countless assortment of names and styles of oyster. It would take forever and a day to try every permutation out there, but it's a fun thing to attempt nonetheless.

Foodies are smart and deeply passionate people. More often than not, they'll put in the time to learn about the food they love so much. Oyster farms not only provide an amazing product but play a key role in educating consumers on the value and benefits of the industry. The enhanced value that comes with knowledge of the source of your food and the process behind making it helps justify the price point. No additives, no preservatives, all-natural, locally sourced, and hand-crafted are terms that are overused these days. But once you've tasted a variety of oysters, you understand the truth of those terms and the distinct and noticeable difference between crafted and processed food. There is nothing quite like visiting an oyster farm, taking a ride on the boat, and witnessing the process first-hand. And then, of course, trying an oyster plucked right out of the water for your enjoyment. Once you connect the taste, the story, and the people, it's easy to shell out the higher price for a plate of oysters, since you know where that money will end up: back with the farmer, to help craft more of those oysters.

"The greatest part about oysters," says Skip Bennett of Island Creek, "is that every one is different. There is always a story behind the oyster. Where it's from, who the grower is, how it got to that person's table in a restaurant or at a person's home."

Now that you know the story of the crafted oyster, hopefully you've grown to appreciate this delicious edible. Whether it's your first or thousandth time enjoying a raw oyster, taking the time to admire the natural beauty of sight, smell, and, ultimately, taste can connect you to an essential wonder from Mother Nature. There are so many sublime and sensational facets to delight in, to appreciate, to discuss, to ponder, and to remember. Each experience is unique. Each oyster subtly different. You're bound to discover something new every time you enjoy an oyster.

But don't forget, it's about the journey *and* the destination. The destination, in this case, is your plate. Happy slurping!

ACKNOWLEDGMENTS

Bushels of gratitude to Dan Crissman for deciding an oyster book was worth salivating over. Thanks for being an oyster fan.

Róisín Cameron, my editor, put the polish on the pearl, and Max Winter's editing accoutrements got the finishing touches just right. I truly appreciate it all.

All the fantastic oyster farms and owners out there that helped make this book possible. It's phenomenal what they do and the passion they have for oysters. A special thanks to Tal Petty, Matt Gregg, Kevin McLaren, Abigail Carroll, Lissa James Monberg, Lane Zirlott, Skip Bennett, Annie MacNamara, Brian Pinsky, Ted Nowakowski, Thad Nowakowski, Mica Verbrugge, Michael Osinski, Cody Mills, and Kate Muirhead for taking the time to answer questions and share their stories.

Shane and the whole magnificent crew at Upstate, past and present. A pearl among oyster venues. Thanks for indulging me with incredible oysters, tasty beverages, endless evenings of conversation, and escapades. It was the incubator for all of this. I am indebted.

To the members of Dinner Club. That night we decided to get oysters for an appetizer and ended up eating 12 dozen. Yeah. 144 oysters. So good. The bartender was so impressed he gave us free champagne. That was spectacular. Thank you for that.

Real Datsun. You know who you are.

To my extended family and all my friends with whom I've eaten oysters. Stop bugging me already with oyster questions. You should know enough about them by now. Much love.

A sincerely special thank you to my great friend Ryan, a foodie soul mate. Wandering into that random new oyster venue that looked tasty and cozy (Upstate) was the beginning of this surreal journey. Thanks for all the adventures over the years and for helping to craft so many fun ideas—oysters and beyond. You'll get that island house soon.

My father can't believe that I eat oysters. Or fathom why I do. This book won't change his mind either. Glad we can both laugh at that fact. My mother enjoys the occasional oyster, especially when I can share the story behind it. Thanks for the eternal support and raising me with an appreciation of food, and an inquisitive mind, that led me to oysters. Having to finish everything on my plate growing up was worth it.

Mały Mieciu—We've been boundless with ideas since we were little. Thanks for the continual support, helping make the proof of concept a reality for all of this, and being an amazing brother.

Jess and Lu—There are too many oyster shells to count for all the good eats we've shared. It's been fodder for the foodie fire. You've both inspired so much. Many thanks and much love for all the fun and support through life's adventures.

The endless and boundless joy that are my nieces and nephews. You're remarkable. The world is your oyster. Find your passion and run with it. Thanks for making the world bright and very easy to be a proud uncle.

A bigger-than-big thank you to my phenomenally talented, insightful, and, most of all, patient agent, Jess Regel. Your belief in the idea and conjuring it out of me was unbelievable. Your guidance through the entire process for a novice writer was exceptional. Your advice was shrewd. Your demeanor was impeccable and elegant. You have a knack for this that's impressive. Thanks for dealing with my roller coaster ride.

I could never thank my wife enough, or hug her enough, for seeing this idea and nudging me, pushing me, shoving me, to create the proposal and the book you're now holding. Your sensibility and stability from start to finish was, is, and always will be, magnificent. When I was lost in the weeds of the creative process, you always managed to pluck a bouquet of amazingness from it all to admire. You are exquisite at every level and appreciated beyond words. Especially for trying the occasional oyster with me and your innate shucking talent. Love you.

For my daughter. You were tucked snug in your mother's womb throughout the writing of this book. Ethereal dreams hopefully swimming in your head before you arrived. You are our first story. You are the best story. You are the story that changed my life in the most amazing way possible. I am so happy you are here. I love you.

INDEX